D1345924

3 3012 00043 4611

Windows

Mary Portas

Windows

The Art of Retail Display

With 252 colour illustrations

To Graham, Mylo and Verity

First published in the United Kingdom in 1999 by Thames & Hudson Ltd, 181A High Holborn, London WC1V 7QX

British Library Cataloguing-in-Publication Data
A catalogue record for this book is available from the British Library

ISBN 0-500-01944-4

Printed and bound in Singapore by C. S. Graphics

Author's Note
My most sincere thanks go to all the many retailers, photographers, stylists, designers and suppliers who have so generously supplied me with their wonderful images. I have made every effort to credit all those concerned, but hope that it will be at least some consolation to anyone omitted to see so many photographs brought together as a tribute to the art of the window-dresser. Any such omissions are greatly regretted.

The photograph of Harvey Nichols, London, on pages 18-19 is by Steve Speller.

Frontispiece ***This reminds me of Horst's famous*** **Vogue** ***cover which featured an eyeliner-swept eye on a white canvas. Shiseido have re-created the power of that image with swollen, red lips pouting towards the glass.*** ***Shiseido, Japan***

Contents

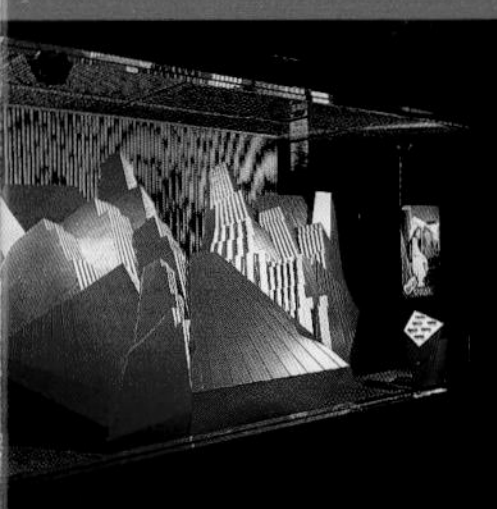

Right *Sculptural city skyscrapers dwarf the intimate product, a powder compact, creating a juxtaposition both striking and intriguing.* **Shiseido, Japan**

Foreword

This is a book for everyone in retailing: it's about what you can do for your windows and what your windows can do for you. Those illuminated spaces that line our pavements are the most underused form of retail advertising: they're the art of the high street. The skill of the artist is to turn the many different sides of life into a visual ensemble, and the skill of the window-dresser is to do just the same, but with a commercial slant. That really *is* a skill, and I'd like people to be able to pick up this book and see how brilliantly and creatively good window design can be used. Window-dressing isn't just about a set that gets crushed at the end of the month and left on a skip; it's a tactical marketing method with the same longevity and branding ability as any advertising campaign.

The pictures in this book are testament to the efforts of the unsung heroes of the display world who create our shop windows. With sore knees and threadbare jeans, noses pressed to the bosoms of cold mannequins, window-dressers work through the night to put a bit of glamour into pedestrian life. I'm not trying to elevate what they do, not trying to make them anything more than window-dressers; all I'm saying is: Recognize their skill and their talent.

I'd like to thank the people who have executed my concepts and ideas, and the teams of people who have believed in me and made it possible for me to create my designs, particularly my team at Yellow Door, and, for their open-mindedness, the directors of Harvey Nichols. It took guts for them to let me leave the store's windows bare one Christmas, or to re-dress the façade of the store as a slum; they were prepared to take risks and that's why they're the retailers they are today. Thanks are due also to Karen Swan MacLeod for her energy and support; to Jonathan Durden, Nick Horswell and David Pattison for their kindness; to Georg Stärk for his wonderful photographs; to Caroline Matcham, Roger Fisher, Mandy Tillet, Clare Bjorklund and Phil Stentiford for making my working days easier and making me laugh and laugh and laugh; to Anna Harvey for first recognizing my work in *Vogue*; and to Mike Potter, for the soundest of advice and his unstinting belief in me.

MARY PORTAS, London, 1999

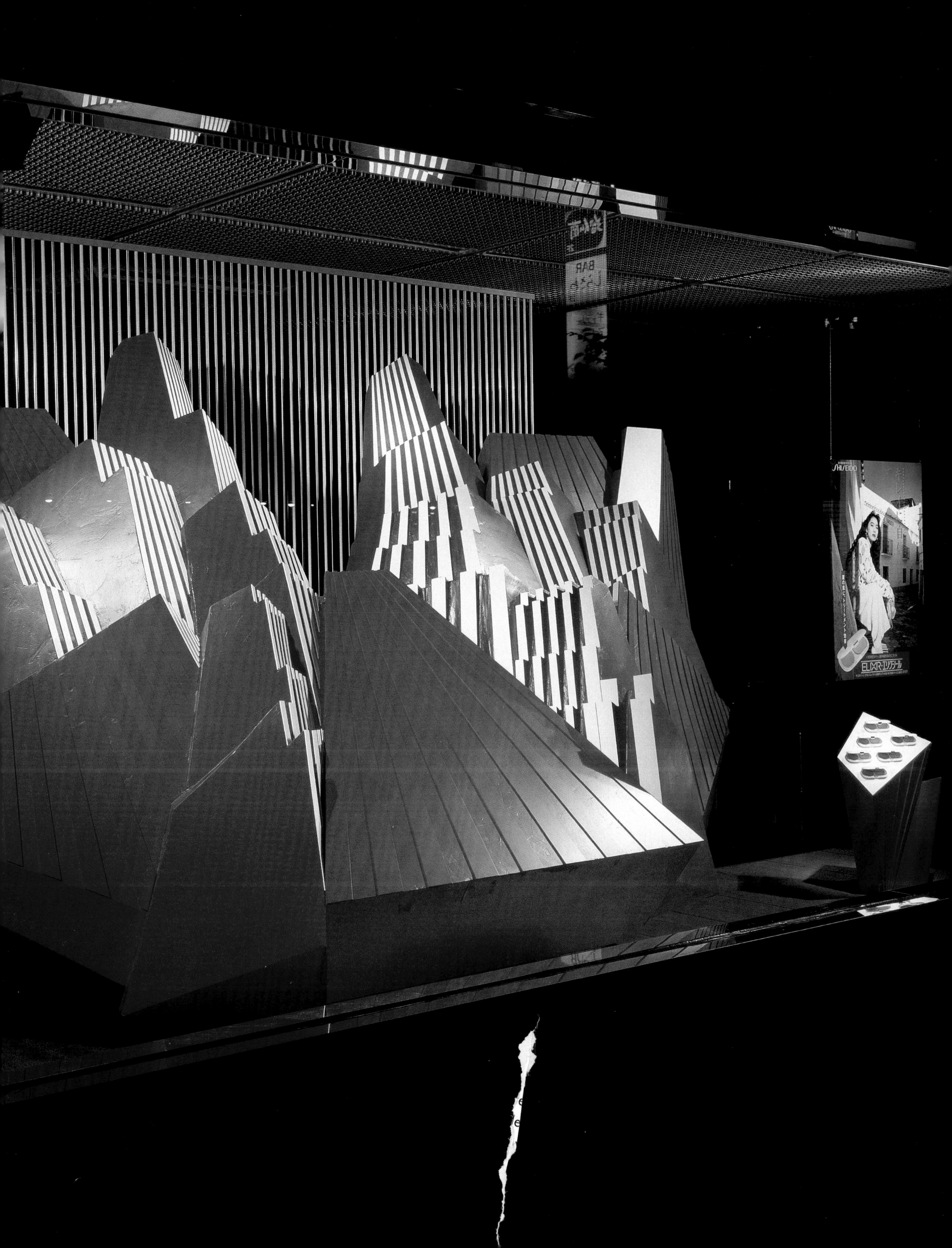
SHISEIDO
夏の肌にトリートメント効果
ELIXIR・エリクシール

Preface

Mirror, mirror, on the wall, who is the fairest of them all? This question has spurred on numerous revolutions in society this century. The quest for youth, health and beauty has affected everything from politics to art to culture: the growing influence of women in politics coincided with shorter skirts and the freeing of women's bodies from corsets; the emergence of the teenager in the 1950s redefined the nuclear family and had an irrevocable impact upon film, art, music and fashion; and the rise of the cult of exercise and cosmetic surgery made preconceptions of age redundant and introduced the notion of life-stages. As the Western World's faith in religion wanes, so the power of beauty increases. Beauty can bring down governments, help charities, ignite feuds, make fortunes. Beauty makes people stop and stare, imprisoning them as it enthrals – witness the double take on the street when a beautiful woman passes, or the crowd that gathers around a portrait in a gallery, or the cult of the model as celebrity. Shop windows are mirrors to reflect the faces of our time; beauty is their currency as they trade in glamour, sophistication, taste, humour, style.

But it wasn't always thus. Shop windows as we know them today – as settings for street theatre and artistic tableaux – are a recent phenomenon dating back to the late 1920s. At their inception at the turn of the century, they were small and functional, simply a means to introduce light into dark, narrow shops. Merchandise would be placed at the back of the window to allow light to shine in unimpeded. The growing availability of plate-glass widened the scope for size and shape and increasingly the merchandise was placed to the fore – windows were transformed into selling tools. As shops grew larger and department stores evolved, the importance of windows grew in direct proportion to their size, enticing customers with refined Art Deco displays that whetted appetites whilst emitting a store's brand image. Already the link between commerce and art had been established, nowhere more so than in France, which is rightly considered the birthplace of the modern window display.

You only have to look at the bustling art scene in Paris to see why. Artists such as Man Ray, Picasso and Duchamp headed the bill, with designers such as Elsa Schiaparelli, who instigated *prêt-à-porter* with her first 'take-out fashion' collection, forging new attitudes and making inroads into modern design. Schiaparelli collaborated with artists – Jean Cocteau embroidered line-sketches on her clothes – and moved design out of its narrowly defined arenas, presenting it commercially to the public. Naturally this approach spilled over into window display. Many artists – Jasper Johns, Robert Rauschenberg and James Rosenquist among them – began their careers in shop-window design.

But it was Salvador Dalí who really made shop windows respectable. Surrealism was all in 1930s Paris, perverting the logic of reality with the chaos of the subconscious; window display was a perfect stage for fluid dreamscape. Dalí was commissioned by the New York store Bonwit Teller to create two window pastiches exploring the myth of Narcissus. One of these, 'Narcissus White', featured a mannequin crying bloody tears, propped in a bath of muddy water and surrounded by hundreds of suspended hands holding mirrors. A narrative on the hideous face of self-love, it was deemed too radical for the store and disassembled. While Dalí was emptying the bathtub, he slipped and it crashed through the glass window out onto Fifth Avenue. Never one to miss an opportunity, he dived through the shattered glass after it; the moment was caught on camera and filled the front pages the next day.

After that, the notion of the shop window as a tame medium was dispelled and a coalition with art was established. Window design followed developments in the art world closely, as Surrealism was gradually replaced by the German design school, the Bauhaus, and its minimalist, steely, utilitarian principles of modernism. The pre-eminence of American architects such as Frank Lloyd Wright and the relocation of the Bauhaus and the architect Ludwig Mies van der Rohe to America in the late 1930s account for New York's replacement of Paris as the home of innovative window display.

Gene Moore was the giant behind New York's reputation. Having started at Bonwit Teller, in 1956 he became Display Director at Tiffany & Co. and stayed for 39 years, gaining cult status for engaging pedestrians with 'hide-and-seek' games and witty puns, always acknowledging art's legacy: a yellow diamond brooch, fashioned as a flower, would be suspended before a beautiful nose in a Daliesque spin, or a collage of gleaming cutlery, arranged in rhythmic patterns, might pay homage to Bauhaus chic. The artistic influence didn't end there. In the course of his reign at Tiffany's, Moore commissioned more than 900 artists to collaborate on his windows, his only stipulation being that they must be unknown.

The one exception to that rule was Andy Warhol, whom Moore had commissioned whilst still at Bonwit Teller. Warhol had by then made his name on the New York art scene, but had continued to work with shop windows having started with a part-time job in the display team at Horne's department store in Pittsburgh when he was still an art student. Exploring the symbiosis between art and commerce, Warhol transplanted his signature style from one artistic medium to another, outlining products and props with his famous graphic line.

Windows were, then, a valid complement – rather than a support system – to contemporary art. But today they fulfil another function as well. Modern marketing and advertising are sophisticated animals that pervade every area of consumer life. Magazines, TV, radio and newspapers all educate the consumer relentlessly, setting new standards, providing new experiences and creating a buyer's market. Shopping in stores isn't the only option these days. Increasingly the customer is invited to shop from home – ordering groceries by e-mail, buying jewelry over the telephone, choosing clothes on the Internet. Now, more than ever, the shop window has to dazzle and seduce to entice customers through the door. Because of the technology that characterizes our modern media, window displays, their inherent simplicity by comparison dated, not high-tech enough, can be overlooked by retailers as mere eye candy. And yet are there any retailers who'd be confident enough to blacken their windows and stonewall pedestrians with an empty façade? It's when you consider just how many people pass a window, compared with the circulation figures of a target-specific magazine or TV programme, that windows come into their own. The opportunity to turn a pedestrian into a customer is there all day every day *and* throughout the night. Turning a window into a high-fidelity promotional tool requires as much sophistication and canniness as any advertising campaign: the concept, the execution, the colour palette, the props and mannequins, and the use of space and lighting all converge to create a dynamic image as powerful as any fashion shoot.

And it is just about image. Windows exist on a higher plane than selling – they're about fantasy and enigma; the bottom line, selling, only kicks in inside the store, so, in all but promotional windows, the product is simply part of the ensemble.

People pass windows very quickly and their attention won't be attracted by a naive brand thrust. Every other store on the block might mirror your windows, as most retailers in the same markets are working with similar merchandise. Customers want individuality. Just as every woman's nightmare is walking into a room and encountering someone in exactly the same dress, every retailer dreads walking down the street and seeing the same window idea being used by a competitor. So revel in the unexpected.

Windows have become the face of Christmas these days; just as fairy tales, mythology and cartoons gave us Santa Claus, elves and living snowmen, so windows spin new fables, depicting maybe an Arabian theme with silks and flying carpets, or perhaps circus performers whose festivity and fantastic contortions are as close to magic as flying reindeer. At Christmas, every TV company sends camera crews to New York to record the festivities. Christmas is increasingly becoming a consumer animal, with cries of 'Buy! Buy! Buy!' twisting the selfless gift-giving philosophy of religion into a secular leisure experience.

Perhaps it is because of the novelty of shopping in cyberspace or on the telephone that the traditional experience of 'going shopping' has been invested with social kudos. 'Want' is very different from 'need', heartening news for the modern retailer as it implies that passers-by are looking for an excuse to step over the threshold; a dynamic window can be all it takes. If all the windows along a high street boasted innovative schemes, dramatically lit and executed with precision, care and pride, it would be like looking at a row of TV sets all switched on, buzzing, vibrant and informing us about the world we live in.

Windows can create their own electricity and hold their own among the levels of technology that we embrace in our everyday lives – it's knowing which buttons to push. When it comes down to it, all window design is ever really about is making the extremes of life a reality. Whether depicted in the chaotic disorder of Surrealism or the practical sobriety of Bauhaus, life is a glorious mix: fun, serious, whimsical, graphic, minimalist, decorative, dramatic and subtle. The skill of the artist – painter, musician, sculptor or display team – is to make these sensations visual and tangible, to make them enter the imagination of the viewer.

It's very difficult to quantify the success of windows, especially as their effect on sales performance can't be measured accurately, but I knew I'd really made my mark at Harvey Nichols when a London tour operator began to ring every month to check our window-display themes so that he could bring his tourist coaches round to have a look. Perhaps the only true test is when customers react to what they see – the windows are, after all, there for them. I've run the gamut: from having a regular customer call me on a car phone as he drove past telling me that these windows were certainly not my best, to the Queen Mother remarking on the windows to the Managing Director of Harvey Nichols at a garden party. The windows exceeded expectations, branding the store and becoming a destination in themselves. So this book is for any business which dares to think that windows don't matter. It's a textbook on the commercial worth of the window-dresser, a wonderful reflection of our culture, a feast for the eyes. Read this book and it'll tell you how to make *your* store the fairest of them all.

Opposite *In this beautifully understated window designed by Naomi Yamamoto, product and prop, bangles and bubbles, are one and the same.* **Shiseido, Japan**

Is It Art?

'All department stores will become museums and all museums will become department stores.'

Andy Warhol

Ask me how I would define art, and I'd start by saying that it's got nothing to do with a canvas, a frame and a picture rail. I consider art to be a dynamic impulse, the tangible product being merely the sum total of an energy that has been channelled into concept and application. For me, art should engage a response, elicit a reaction, initiate an interaction on a moral, a religious or even just an aesthetic level. I am calling this chapter 'Is It Art?' because when I was at Harvey Nichols our windows did just that. So many people got a thrill from them; it was a delight to watch passers-by openly laughing at the windows, laughing with us and reacting to them; standing and taking time out of their busy lives to enjoy something that they might not otherwise have encountered. So according to this definition, yes, windows can be art. When creative energy is your brief, what's the difference between exhibiting in a gallery, designing a stage set or going into a window? The aptitude and the creativity required aren't any less – the difference is geography. Think back to the sleeping woman exhibit at the Serpentine Gallery in London when Tilda Swinton slept in a glass box for eight hours a day on view to the general public; the premise is, if it's an art gallery, then it must be art. But what if you give that art a commercial motive? Cue Selfridges, who applied a similar theme to their windows, with living people surfing the net, reading, cooking and, of course, sleeping. Living exhibits. Glass walls. The same idea but filed under different headings: department store; art gallery. Perspective was the only variable.

But I do understand the urge to question the validity of windows within the realm of art, because traditional boundaries delineating art have shifted. Traditionally, only art for art's sake has been regarded as the legitimate vehicle for the true artistic impulse, yet contemporary artists like Charles Ray, Tracey Emin and Jake & Dinos Chapman have made blatantly contradictory, and controversial, moves into the commercial sector. Indeed at the Royal Academy's 'Sensation' exhibition in London in 1997, the parallels between modern art and window display were striking, with Sarah Lucas borrowing display's visual gags and Damien Hirst encasing his work in glass vitrines. Why this route? Because the hands-off élitism that's been synonymous with the scene for so long has, by keeping people at arm's length, brought about that scene's nemesis; for art to fulfil its role as a stimulant, it needs an audience, but how many people actually go to art galleries? In a discussion on the sculptor Anish Kapoor's work, Miuccia Prada, of the Italian designer house Prada, said: 'Art is getting away from its traditional setting...We are beginning to see it all around us. It is not just a visual thing but something in many dimensions – a physical, spiritual experience.' And I think she's right. Like so many other elements of modern culture – music, literature, fashion – innovation is pushing up from the grass roots; in the art world, a dumbing down of the ivory-tower mentality is taking place, with new mavericks taking art out of the gallery's controlled environment, and pushing it at people where it's least expected.

One thing I learnt at art college is that everything connects. To today's generation whose buzzword is 'lifestyle', tackling art on a lateral level picks out these common threads. Take the London restaurant The Square, where Philip Howard's food is served amongst Deborah Layon's modernist canvases – art's new impetus to socialize, to integrate, represents a move towards merging stimulants, blending differing art forms into a cohesive genre. The international retailer Joseph, for example, sells PVC jeans in his boutiques and lattes in the café, whilst displaying couture in his windows. Likewise John Galliano, the Paris-based designer, creates a pastiche that's as artistically valid as any Degas or Cézanne, whether he places his audience in 1950s wing-tip Cadillacs, or a circus ring or a boudoir. In all these cases, 3-D interactive art is used as a backdrop to the product – Layon's paintings to Howard's Caesar salad, the couture to Joseph's coffee, the cars to Galliano's bias-cut dresses – and, as a result, the art has been rendered as valid, and more importantly as relevant, as the product. Apply this approach to windows and the question arises: Do they, as art, deliver something greater than all the tactical strategies a business is trying to manipulate? You only have to look at the Christmas windows in New York to see the excitement of the lines of people queueing with families and children to realize that windows are actually entertainment. They're something bigger than just selling. Half the people you see standing outside Saks Fifth Avenue or Barneys or Bergdorf Goodman won't be shopping there – they've just come for the excitement. It's fun to think that windows can bring a touch of glamour and a bit of theatre to the streets, but they also enhance the store's image and compound its ambition of branding and creating an aspiration.

So art can be image, it can be energy, and it can also be essence. I once did a great window themed on London. I took the lions from Trafalgar Square – something that everyone from Japanese tourists to City office-workers associates with London – and cast them in bright orange, with their manes as the River Thames. Boats floated down the manes, and on the lions' hind legs I put a wonderful car clamp (parking clamps had become the bane of London's drivers in the 1980s). There was a royal purple backdrop, and to top it all, flocks of orange pigeons flying everywhere. That window *was* London, interpreted in a slightly obtuse way perhaps, but it identified elements that were present in ordinary people's lives and twisted them into something unique. And I think that's ultimately what art's aim should be: to offer a reinterpretation, to propose a new angle on the familiar, to produce something brighter, loftier and more controversial than the mundane that we know and live through. My leitmotif is humour and it's rewarding to me to think that I've put smiles on some London faces and a witty charm on London's face. Art is about being a part of your time; by the same reckoning, windows let you put a face to the *Zeitgeist* – and that face is commerciality wrapped up with style. I agree with Brian Sewell, the art critic of the London *Evening Standard*: 'I argue that some of the most site-specific art is in the windows of Harvey Nichols; they are infinitely more exciting than anything that appears in the Tate.' Well, I would, wouldn't I?

Above *Dynamic, modern and witty, everything in this set by Naomi Yamamoto explodes with energy and impact. The unlikely 'prop' echoes both the shape and the vibrant colour of the product.* **Shiseido, Japan**

Opposite *Owing a debt to Warhol and Pop art, this window, again by Naomi Yamamoto, is sexy, alluring and daring, all characteristics associated with red lipstick, and with the women who wear it.* **Shiseido, Japan**

Above *This fantastic carbon sculpture by Thomas Heatherwick was the last window I commissioned for Harvey Nichols. It twines and snakes around the building as though it's alive, diving through the panes of glass into the window sets. This design was incredibly difficult to instal, but the interest it aroused justified everything.* ***Harvey Nichols, London***

'...what's the difference between exhibiting in a gallery, designing a stage set or going into a window?'

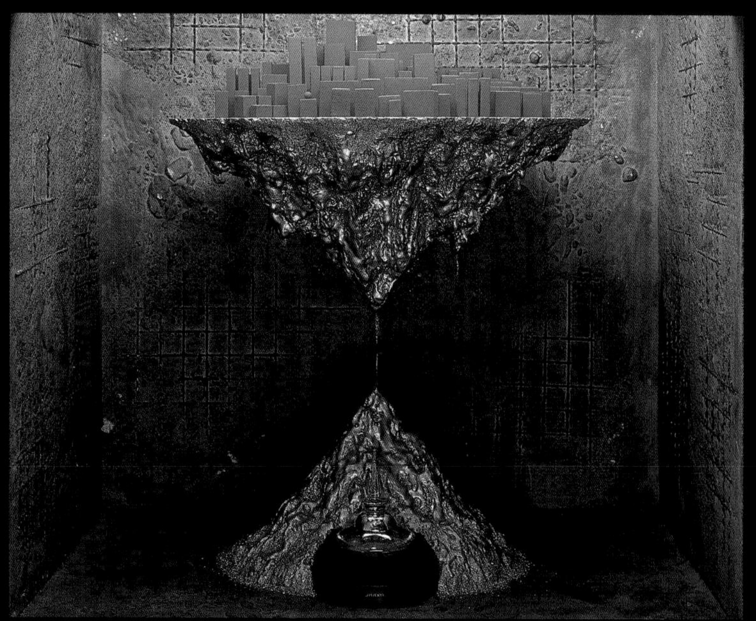

Above *Hard versus soft; aggression versus passivity: this display trades in extremes. Skincare and anti-ageing creams are the holy grail that justifies such fighting talk.*
Shiseido, Japan

Opposite above *Flighty and flimsy, sheaves of paper are scattered like a flurry of doves, as the smooth hardness of the orb makes its impact. There's a great use of form and density, creating an artwork from the most mundane of materials.*
Shiseido, Japan

Opposite below left *I love the ordered chaos in this display, which, like the others on this spread, is by Naomi Yamamoto. The product, by comparison, stands alone, hypnotic in its isolation.* **Shiseido, Japan**

Opposite below right *The angularity of the icy blue skyscrapers contrasts with the irregularity of the golden cave beneath, presenting perfume as a subterranean fuel for the senses.* **Shiseido, Japan**

'...taking art out of the gallery's controlled environment, and pushing it at people where it's least expected

Top and above *Vital, moody, elegant and clever, these Japanese displays, designed by Masaru Takeuchi, are based on iconic works of art by Botticelli and Modigliani – life imitating art with great ingenuity. Both designs are guaranteed to stop any passer-by.* **Central Park, Japan**

Opposite *This window by Peter Rank differs from the previous two in that it is a re-creation in 3-D of a well-known painting. Here, the shop's merchandise has become an integral part of Dalí's composition.* **Tiffany & Co., Munich**

Opposite and below *There's a spectacular sense of movement and flow in this display, as the still-life plastic bottles meld into organic jellyfish. It's just so clever. The window feels clean and vital yet subtle, intimating that this is a sophisticated retailer with a highly refined image.* **Central Park, Japan**

'They're something bigger than just selling.' ***'They're something bigger than just selling.***

'They're something bigger than just selling.' *'They're something bigger than just selling.'*

'...So art can be image, it can be energy, and it can also be essence.'

Above *A clever visual pun on 'classical' music adds a spark of self-deprecating humour to the monotony of selling bland silver or black boxes from a window. And I like the fact that she's locked into her own serene world with another buzzing around her.* **Sony, New York**

Opposite above *A face that sells? Turning the cover shot on its head, the ugliness of this face and the crudity of the rope enhance the desirability of the sunglasses in an intriguing and unexpected way.* **Joël Name, New York**

Opposite below left *This window plays on the modern consumer's conceptions of contemporary fashion – black, minimalist and slinky. The mannequins echo the shape of the giant ceramic pots in a simple yet unusual display.* **Daffy's, New York**

Opposite below right *Again, a great synergy between the painting and the mannequins forces the eye to bob between the two in this display. None of the figures are real, yet each is realistic; none are overtly dynamic but there's plenty of life in them.* **Mitchells of Westport, USA**

"...merging stimulants, blending different art forms..."

Above *The scenes painted as the backdrop appear, at first glance, to be three-dimensional. The clenched fists and steel armchairs reflect each other's references to strength and masculinity, with the two mannequins bracing the scene like gatekeepers.* **Ka Da We, Berlin**

'...merging stimulants, blending different art forms...'

Above *These huge stone carvings are artistic sculptures in themselves. Their heavy and oblique features emphasize the lightness, transparency and fragility of the scarves in a way that less extreme opposites could not effect. It's an amazing mix.*
Nicole Miller, New York

AND YOURS, SARAH
IS PLAYING IN A
BALENCIAGA BALLGOWN.

FLOUR

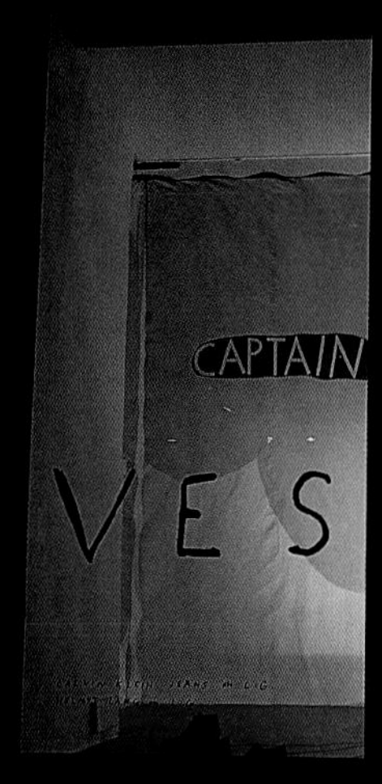
CAPTAIN
VES

good

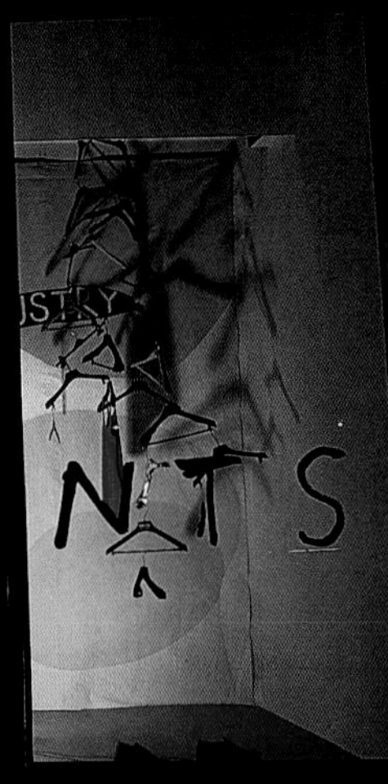
OF INDUSTRY

Opposite above *A perfect display for the Soundbite Generation. Dickins & Jones have created elegant, mutant icons which take their cue from the Pop art movement. The cartoon-like visual language invites you to take part.* **Dickins & Jones, London**

Opposite below left *This mannequin's bread head is grotesque but he is dressed in a beautiful twill jacket, like a manicured traveller. The swag-bag of billowing silk ties conjures up memories of childhood adventure stories.* **Paul Stuart, New York**

Opposite below right *I asked Paul Davis to sketch these massive canvases for a menswear promotion, expressing masculinity and men – men's thoughts, men's lives. We skewed the straightness of the scenes with word plays and puns, and let the sheer energy, technicolor and wit deliver their impact.* **Harvey Nichols, London**

Above *I'm completely stopped by this window by Simon Doonan. There are so many layers to peel back; everything is echoed as a multiple of two – the two-tone colours, the dual heads in 2-D, the model and her reflection. There's an illusion of quiet activity and hidden intimacy: you're forced to explore.* **Barneys, New York**

Above *Dwarfed by this V for Victory, the product is bathed in a pool of light. This window, designed by Celia Lindsell, shows that British Tiffany is a retailing success story with energy and attitude.* **Tiffany & Co., London**

Opposite *In this second window designed by Celia Lindsell, the unlikely combination of valuable jewelry and mundane household materials shaped into luxury goods is both beautifully crafted and fascinating. But irreverence towards the product is something only the most established of luxury retailers can pull off.* **Tiffany & Co., London**

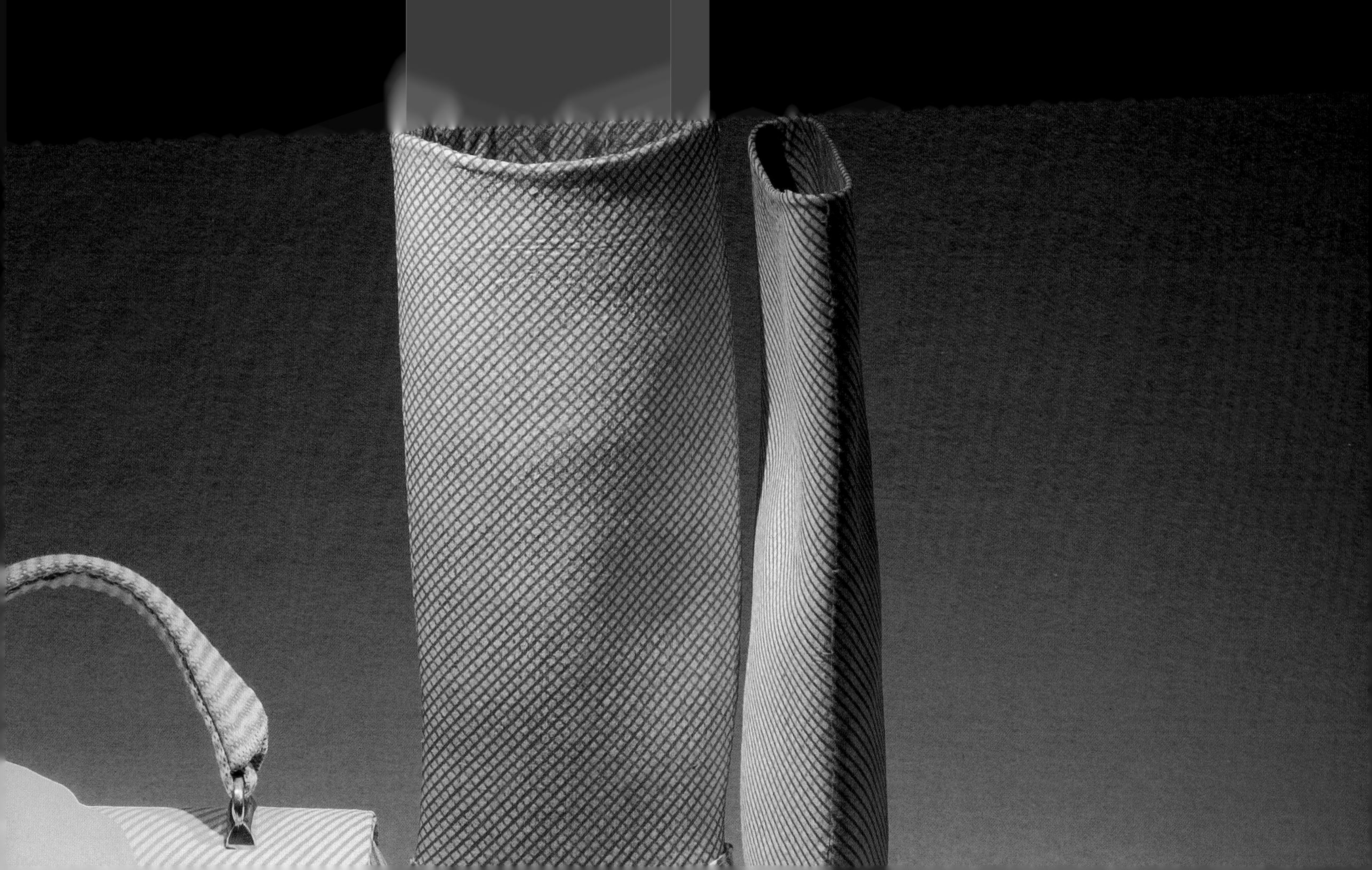

Opposite *If you know your product and your customers, you don't need to spend much to draw them in. This window proves the point, spelling out the notion of Happy Hour with relaxed, easy-going tropical images and brightly coloured letters painted to resemble a pinball machine.* **Anon, Zurich**

Budgets

B
A
C
R

> **'With windows, you have just a few seconds to get someone's attention; visual humour is the most effective way, transcending the barriers of both language and budget.' Paul Smith**

I've often drawn the parallel that if eyes are the windows to the soul, so shop windows reveal the soul of the store. They communicate its very essence in an unblinking front that stands constant long after trading hours have ceased and the last customer has left. They're the most economic form of advertising a retailer has, working on a round-the-clock shift even when you're not there. And they can work for you even when *they're* not there. I once executed a window scheme which saw each window painted a different colour and kept completely bare, save for a notice saying that the money that would otherwise have been spent on the windows had been donated to charity. Admittedly, it was a proposition only open to a big retail operation with an established brand which could afford to take such a big risk as actually blanking out its identity; but those 'non-windows' gained coverage in four national newspapers and demonstrated the unlimited advertising power of windows in a store's operations.

Windows may be the poor relations of brash, million-pound advertising campaigns, but they still operate on a sliding scale of budgets which can run into the thousands for the prestigious, big-name retailers. But a dynamic window isn't necessarily synonymous with a big budget. I've often found that the most inventive windows are the result of limited budgets, those where you have had to stretch your imagination in creative terms rather than financial. In the last chapter we looked at creative *élan* from a theoretical standpoint and how perceptions of modern art are shifting to incorporate the artistic impulse, whatever its form. In this chapter, we'll look at how to deploy that energy in its purest, most literal sense, without resorting to financial excess.

Inevitably, budget determines scale, but success rests on approach rather than size. I always work from the premise that less money doesn't mean compromise; essentially you should build a story up, rather than think of a big idea and pare it down. Quality is the one thing money can buy – great finishes, top mannequins, 3-D bespoke props – but if the concept or idea isn't there, quality can't help. One thing to remember is that if you're working to a very minimalist scale with little or no visual layers, changing products more regularly will stimulate those thousands of passers-by on their way to and from work. I make several analogies with the theatre throughout this book, but when it comes to finish, the theatrical approach is best avoided: sets that look grand from 30–40ft away are, when you stand close to them on stage, very crude and naive. With windows, I've seen people literally pressing their noses against the glass, just inches away; you can't afford to skimp over finish. Basic maintenance and levels of pride speak volumes about your attitude to your business and your customers. Keep the windows clean; put down a great fabric floor; steer clear of old, bashed props and flat, boring graphics; use coloured ribbons for hanging rather than nylon. There are countless ways to upgrade the polish of a budget window, but nothing will work without imagination. I remember a truly innovative window design by the restaurant Villandry in London's Marylebone High Street. Brown, curled-up oak leaves had been stuck along the outside glass of the windows to great effect, giving the restaurant a very domestic, artisan air, and at what cost? Just the time it took to sweep the pavement. At Harvey Nichols I directed a window scheme which featured Coca-Cola bottles filled with coloured water and arranged as the American flag: the essence of Americana in a bottle for the cost of two packets of food dye. Both windows are examples of refined concepts and simple, graphic application, and neither could be considered makeshift because they worked within a framework that fitted the budget.

Besides unbridled creativity and lateral thinking, there are other elements you can use to communicate to great effect: humour, quirkiness and surrealism, the 'Three Graces' of the budget window. To me, being inventive means going slightly off the wall, exaggerating an element of a concept, and humour invariably proves to be a tactical offensive which breaks down barriers and the pedestrian stonewall. I've seen some great budget windows which have garnered attention – and customers – just because they were funny. I remember an optician who had placed a row of mops in a window and placed sunglasses on their tousled heads in a surreal spoof; Butler & Wilson decorated a life-size cut-out of Dame Edna Everidge's sidekick Madge the Badge with ornamental earrings and necklaces; but possibly the best was the Paul Smith store in London's Covent Garden, which used a spiky rubber bumble ball in a Paul Smith bag, switched on and left to bounce around the window until the batteries died. Covent Garden is a huge tourist magnet and the comedy of the window spoke an international language.

Shop windows welcome visitors to a town or city, playing the role of host – the smiling face that greets the passer-by, the wind of change that delivers new seasons. Windows are not about money but energy, pride and image, and if you can use those qualities to define your business, you don't need to leave it to money to do the talking.

Opposite *Colour is a strong ally when you're working to a budget. Here, pillars and urns of apples and a chair painted apple-green are soothing and crisp, and the idea of being surrounded by fresh fruit is strangely decadent, even if the outlay isn't. Witty sophistication doesn't need to come with a hefty price tag.* **Blumen Reich, Düsseldorf**

Top *There are no props in this window, only the products stacked in rhythmic order, yet they create a visually exciting collage, playing with colour stories and textures that draw the eye across in a logical pattern.* **Printemps, Paris**

Centre *When your products are miniature works of art, you don't need a budget at all. This delightful display is so full of pride, workmanship and charm that the skill is tangible.* **Bakery Bertschinger, Zurich**

Below *Fresh as a daisy, this beautiful, simple and spring-like display plays on the organic quality of the shell necklaces; the overall effect is one of healthiness, vitality and beauty.* **Falaffa, Zurich**

GLORIA CUBANA
DE
C.E.G.
HABANA
BASTA PASTA
BASTA PASTA
BASTA PASTA

'...windows reveal the soul of the store...'

Above *Variety is clearly the spice of this shop and that message comes across loud and clear. The window hasn't cost anything to produce, and yet the shop's strength has been concisely identified.* **Carter's Nuts, New York**

Opposite above *I love these Art Deco colours and the way the gloopy opaqueness of the painted props is contrasted with the clear-glass bottles. Placing some bottles on their sides introduces new shapes without the need for any extra props, whilst the ever-so-masculine pipes and cigars keep the scheme smoky and gentlemanly.* **Anon, Zurich**

Opposite below *Take something out of its environment and you're forced to look again. Associating pasta with coffee brings out the social, on-the-go slant of the coffee bar, a new effect achieved without having to buy in any props.* **Basta Pasta, New York**

'...work from the premise that less money doesn't mean compromise...'

Above left *Safety in numbers. The mass of irregular, stark orange, pinpointed with a stray purple, grabs attention. The one white trainer sits cleanly, promoting itself as the definitive product, separate from the herd.* **JD Sports, London**

Above right *Find a humorous slant on your business – it's an effective way of reassuring the potential customer as it intimates knowingness and confidence.* **Hairdresser Alfi, Zurich**

Opposite *This window clearly demonstrates the graphic effect of colour and pattern repeats. Wrapping everything in stock paper has cost little, but the crisp neatness of the execution and the consistent square shapes show that thought and care lie behind the finished design.* **Scribbler, London**

Top *The appeal of this well-established retailer is universal; there's no need for John Lewis to rely on attracting passing trade. The powerful primary shades break up the monotony of the Identikit rows in a window which shows great confidence in the product.* ***John Lewis, London***

Centre *As part of a multiple, this retailer needs to keep window schemes simple and refined. The FCUK badge is so loaded with energy and attitude that this is easy to achieve.* ***French Connection, London***

Below *These chicken coops are decorative and amusing in their new incarnation as containers for a random selection of fruit, clothing and knick-knacks. Hardly any styling or money is required, just a sense of the ridiculous and an understanding of what works.* ***c.i.t.e, New York***

Opposite *Colour is a great asset in a budget window, and colour-blocking is particularly powerful. The solidity of the colours contrasts with the fragility of the glass. Graphic and strong, it keeps the eye low, on the product. This window would have been great for selling shoes.* ***Heinemann, Düsseldorf***

'...a dynamic window isn't necessarily synonymous with a big budget.'

970
850
850
650
695
650
695

'...windows are not about money but energy, pride and image.'

Above *This scene of urban decay – bricks and a discarded TV set – gives the product the street cred so crucial for success in this market. Although several interesting props have been used here, the styling ensures that the right mood of disarray comes across.* **Jamarico, Zurich**

Opposite top and centre *I love the way the solidity of the shoes is combined with the flighty parrot feathers in a happy juxtaposition of elements: earth and air.* **J. Fenestrier, Paris**

Opposite below *This autumnal display cost the time it took to sweep the pavement. There's terrific symmetry and order in the shoe arrangements and the crunchy, fallen leaves contrast beautifully with the conker-smooth leather.* **Tizian, Berlin**

UTURE
Perrier

Above *I love the linear simplicity of this display. There's a clear logic directing the scheme, and the strict styling of the products removes the need for many props. An effective seasonal window to sell the product without compromising on style or budget.* **Henri Bendel, Chicago**

Opposite *Mineral water has become a chic fashion accessory. Mixing one of the essentials of life with the transitory world of high fashion was a stroke of marketing genius. The legend H'EAUTE COUTURE wittily underlines the message.* **Liberty, London**

Opposite *Rising high like techno-blue skyscrapers, the ultraviolet lights used in this display create a sense of space and light. Styling is tight: the company's designer, Tom Ford, is known for his strict editing. There's nothing extraneous in this window.*
Gucci, New York

Space and Props

1998

'The model is chosen around a concept but it's the use of space and props that captures and accentuates the character I want to create. The product is my main focal point, from beginning to end, but I always work with a decorator and we adapt space and props to tell the story.'

Mario Testino, photographer

'Why me?' Two little words. The universal call of crisis and despair everywhere. Everywhere, that is, except in retailing where they're a call to arms, a mantra chanted by astute retailers anxious to keep their business ahead of the competition. Retailers have traditionally operated on the received wisdom of giving the customer a reason to want the product and nurturing the want to buy it, but it's a saturated market where other stores are working with the same or similar merchandise, so in real terms, the question should be: 'Why should they want to buy *from me?*'

Windows have to be the first link in the chain to effect that reason why, because beyond necessity purchases, the product alone will not sell. There has to be a depth, a story, attached to the product which will capture the imagination, and, it follows, the credit cards, of passers-by. As we discussed in the chapter on budgets, humour is an effective weapon in this, as is colour which we will come to later; in fact any medium which appeals to the individual should be regarded as a valid tool. But a window design doesn't necessarily need to involve or include the product. In fact, creating a theme too literally around it is a false start because the competition may be working to the same brief. It's best to look instead to props and clever use of space for the most innovative and unique ways of defining your business's image, attracting target customers and answering the 'Why me?' question.

There are a number of decisions to make at the outset, and one is the role of the props – whether they're going to be the authority in the window and override everything else, how much interplay there should be between space and merchandise, and which values the props will attach to the product. In essence props are the key players in the window because you can use them to create a language, a drama, that is unique to your business. Think of your props as the product's DNA – they fashion its character and identity, and render it unique. The hardest part of this process is deciding what the prop should be and kicking off. An empty window is just as menacing as a sheet of blank paper, but logical exploration of what the product is about – twisting its interpretations, going off on tangents that could owe a debt to wordplay or historical associations – is the best way forward. Literal, lateral or colour-based schemes will present themselves, but even then the equation can be difficult to balance. So often, great ideas on paper look somehow dislocated when you fashion them and put them in the window – the dimensions aren't quite right, the finish doesn't work, the colour's slightly wrong. I once saw a dreadful display in a menswear shop with a dartboard with two darts on top; you could see the thought processes: 'What interests men? Ah yes, darts.' The desperation behind it was tangible; it was too literal and too stereotyped. The cleverness lies in using a prop which might not have any direct relevance to the merchandise, and yet, when the two are combined, they hang together in the window. With propping, some of the simplest things are the most graphic. I remember a window where someone had suspended hundreds of dry-cleaner's basic metal hangers from the ceiling, which just twisted and turned, and said 'fashion' and 'clothes' with great authority.

But although, as there, less was more, I'm equally supportive of the 'more is more' approach. Sometimes you can do a slightly chaotic window where the eye is distracted over many areas and it's a feast of layers and elements of surprise – every time you come back you see something new. This method rests very heavily on superb styling to ensure that it doesn't look like a jumble; editing down icons to only those which are central to the scheme will ensure that the window has space. Relevance, closely followed by harmony, should be the watchwords at this stage – if something isn't easy on the eye, the story isn't clear. This juggling act of balancing props and space is vital. I always feel sorry for the multiples because this is where independent or smaller shops and boutiques have the edge. At Harvey Nichols I would regularly tweak the schemes to perfection, days and weeks after they had been put in the windows, but with the multiples – who are dealing with up to 400 shops – that kind of attention to detail is an unrealistic luxury. Invariably you have to scale down the ideas and simplify the grouping, but unfortunately the multiples tend to compromise their props – rather than their story scale – and just throw in a flat graphic and a torso. It's the dirge of the high street. I'm convinced that if you blanked out their shop names, nobody could identify them. For multiples, keep the scale down and the prop quality up. As with small budgets, the practical limitations of executing a display are no excuse for compromise.

To compromise is to undercut the vital role of the prop in spinning a unique interpretation on the product. Essentially this works in one of two ways. One is that props can be used to attach specific values to the product to underpin the brand message and speak to the consumer. Look at what polo boots did for Ralph Lauren; remember how Levi's latched onto a great old mahogany rocking chair to make their point that some things improve with age. In the short term and most relevant to windows, using a prop in this way makes it a unique selling proposition that gives your product the edge; in the longer term and with strategic marketing and advertising, the values lent by the prop can become synonymous with the product, and ultimately, as with Ralph Lauren, your signature. The other element is that the prop can point out the merchandise's direction or end use. One of my favourite windows sprung up around an accessories promotion. Accessories are notoriously difficult to display because they're small and tend only to work as a part of the sum. But we created a papier-mâché pastiche of the animal kingdom dressing up: bats flying down with umbrellas à la Mary Poppins; rows of meerkats with Jean-Paul Gaultier sunglasses; octopuses in hats; and Lucy the Caterpillar wearing Donna Karan hosiery on each of her many legs. The props pointed out the end use of each category of accessory in a way that was fun, innovative and eye-catching. Those windows became a talking-point not only around London but also in the Harvey Nichols boardroom, because I sold every single prop. And if that window balanced the monthly spreadsheets, it wasn't just because I'd fashioned fantasies from paste and soggy newspaper. It was because first I stopped to ask 'Why me?'

'In essence props are the key players in the window...you can use them to create a language, a drama, that is unique to your business.'

Above and opposite *It's interesting to see how the props mirror the poses of the mannequins, carrying themselves with haughty airs and sculpted silhouettes. The flagstone flooring and striped fabrics in this window by Paul Muller are prevented from appearing busy by the large amounts of space between the mannequins.*
Liberty, London

'...Think of your props as the product's DNA...'

Above *The lighting and use of space in this window are simply wonderful. The single mannequin is refined and spare in its silhouette, keeping the products, and therefore the focus of attention, within its parameters.* **Bergdorf Goodman, New York**

Above *In contrast to many other schemes which draw the eye along the window, these sensual silk cushions have been perfectly plumped and balanced to create a vertical line that draws the eye up to the mannequin above. The absence of other objects around the cushions keeps the window light and full of space.* **Versace, New York**

'...they fashion its character and identity, and render it unique.'

Above *Sometimes emptiness can create a sense of expectation. In this instance, the absolute simplicity of the dress demands merely a red carpet and some space to create its impact. Enough said.* **Calvin Klein, New York**

Above *There's a very clear thought process at work here, associating the lightness of the diaphanous robe with the glass marbles. The spacing between the two entities increases that sense of freedom and the lighting is muted, producing an almost mystical quality.* **Saks Fifth Avenue, New York**

Left *These landmark buildings, including the Washington Square Arch and the Flatiron Building, are incorporated so beautifully into the mannequins' masks that they lend an air of mystery both cosmopolitan and gently surreal to the display.*
Saks Fifth Avenue, New York

'...humour is an effective weapon...a window design doesn't necessarily need to involve or include the product

Above *The tension created by using fragile milk bottles as the foundation for a display is complemented by the stark contrast between the white of the milk and the black of everything else, including the bottle tops.* **Heinemann, Düsseldorf**

Opposite top left and below *These voluptuous edible tableaux in the windows of Demel speak for themselves: plenty of other virtuoso examples of the cake-maker's art are available inside.* **Demel, Vienna**

Opposite top right *A jumble of plastic Barbie and Ken figures is humorously juxtaposed with some fine jewelry. A prop doesn't have to have a logical link to the product; if a display engages a response, it works.* **Bucherer, Berlin**

'As with small budgets, the practical limitations o

Above *Here, the mannequin is used to inject a little light relief into the window scheme. The amusing futility of wearing sunglasses with a completely bandaged head engages the attention of the passer-by.* **Paco Rabanne, Paris**

executing a display are no excuse for compromise.'

Above *The simple formula of bringing the sleeve design of Pink Floyd's* The Division Bell *to life is a striking and successful way to get customers into the shop.* **Sony, New York**

Following pages *An audacious display which says to the consumer, 'This is how you live your life, and our products are an essential part of it.'* **Sony, New York**

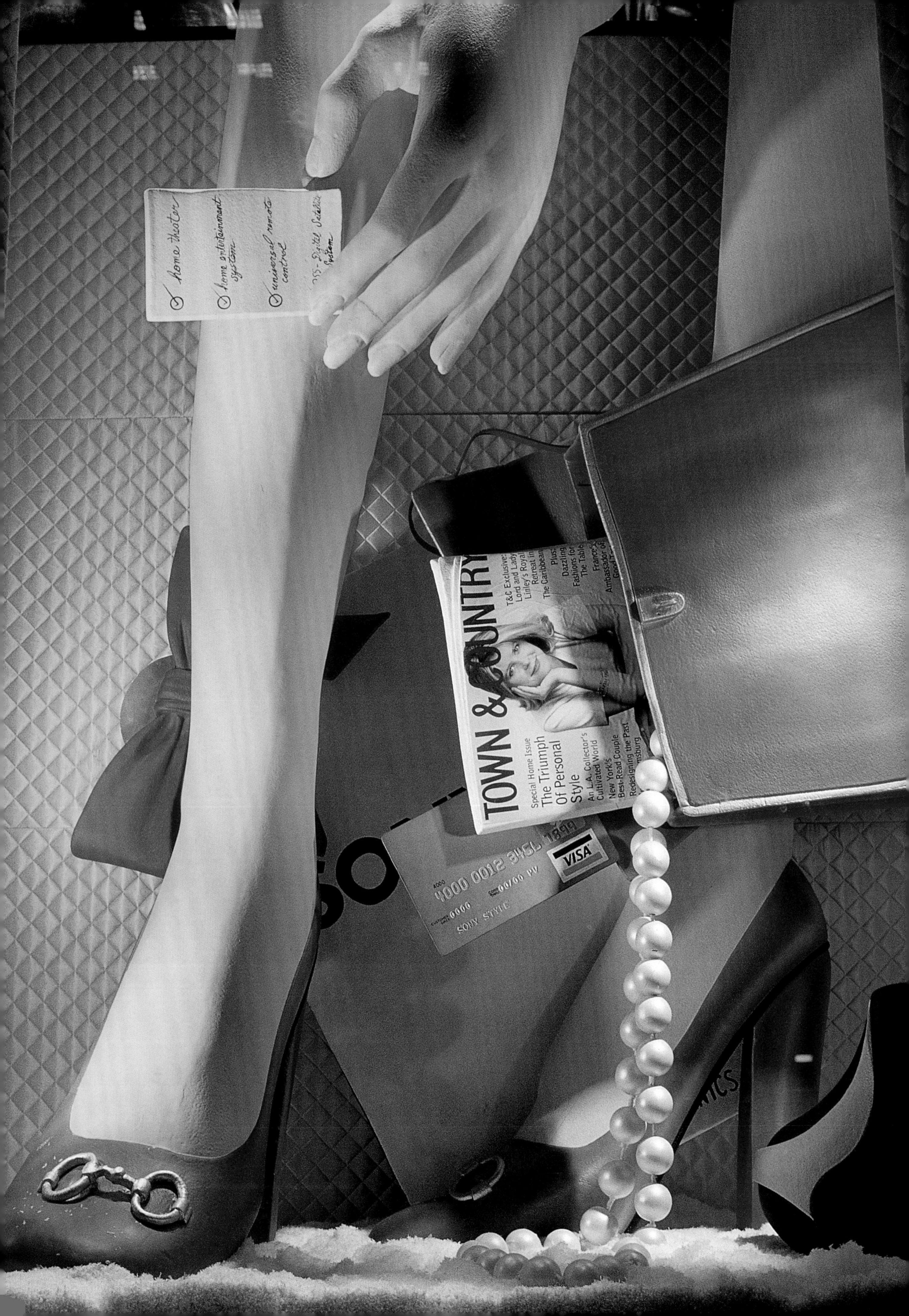
home theater
home entertainment system
universal remote control
DSS-Digital Satellite System
TOWN & COUNTRY
T&C Exclusive: Lord and Lady Linley's Royal Retreat in The Caribbean
Plus: Dazzling Fashions for The Table
Special Home Issue
The Triumph Of Personal Style
An L.A. Collector's Cultivated World
New York's Best-Read Couple
Redesigning the Past
VISA
SONY STYLE

George
Inaugural Issue
John Kennedy talks to George Wallace
President Madonna
Carr on
Mark Leyner
SONY
SONY
Link

Above left *Suspending everything from the ceiling like this really adds to the feeling of lightness and space. The lettering is clear and distinct and gets its branding message across, allowing the boots hanging from the metalwork tendrils to do the fancy footwork, so to speak.* **Tootsi Plohound, New York**

Above right *The draping, linear qualities of these fabrics place a streamlined emphasis on the display. The shoes, placed ankle and toe together so precisely, add to the feeling of elegant restraint and harmony.* **Ferragamo, New York**

Opposite *This sculpted window is the epitome of placement – the placement of props and product. It's precise, geometric and clean. Everything is perfectly balanced, with plenty to look at and plenty of breathing space.* **Cole Haan, New York**

Above *This story – magnifying the vegetable theme that decorates the chinaware – follows a logical connection between product and prop. Vivid colours, giant proportions and an element of the absurd work together to create an arresting display.*
Harvey Nichols, London

Opposite left and right *Tiffany's communication platform – a synthesis of the everyday and the exquisite – is displayed to perfection in these windows by Celia Lindsell. They enhance the brand's standing far more than if the products were placed in opulent surroundings.* **Tiffany & Co., London**

Right *Light, space and texture work together in this window to create a welcoming scene that is rich, serene and soft. The mannequin's relaxed pose adds to the aura of well-being that this display by Sam Joseph exudes.* **Macy's, New York**

Following four pages *This sequence demonstrates how products and props can be layered into a collage of images, colours and textures. Strict styling keeps order within the displays, and prevents an overload of messages.* **Barneys, New York**

MACY'S
FLOWER SHOW
APRIL 9TH - APRIL 22ND HERALD SQUARE

BELVEST
3RD
LUCIANO BARBERA
3RD
CANTARELLI
6TH

BARNEYS NEW YORK
COLLECTION

KING of the
"Beat begat mod and
mod begat hippie and
hippie begat punk and
punk begat grunge..."
MUSEUM
HOT LINE to
our disembodied
HEROPOET
dead Saint
WORMS
CONTINENTAL DIVIDE

NO
SQUARES
ANY
EXIT
GO
CURVES

Opposite *This display shows how variations of tone can add depth to a single colour. Purple is historically associated with power. The sensuality and softness of the velvet dress add to the sense of luxury and sumptuousness, and the bubbles and the dramatic backlighting are perfectly refined, light-of-touch and elegant.*
Saks Fifth Avenue, New York

'More than other formal characteristics, colour has seemed to most of us to speak directly and unambiguously [a good deal of capital has been made from this assumption, not least in the marketing of goods].'

John Gage, COLOUR AND CULTURE, 1993

Imagine a world without colour, a universe in which everything is black and white, and you quickly begin to see the world in terms of totality and extremes. Colour gives the world personality and depth. It's a tremendously emotive catalyst which differing cultures, religions and superstitions have endowed with widely divergent significances and associations. Fuschia pink, for example, is associated with both virility and madness; green is alternately considered a bad omen or a token of fertility; and white can signal either surrender on the battlefield or unsurrendered virginity in a wedding dress. These conflicting suppositions are based on subjective beliefs alone, yet there is a scientific basis to colour rationalizations. It has been quantifiably proven that colour elicits a physiological response, with the eye reacting most quickly to bold colours like orange, red and yellow. Many businesses utilize this knowledge in their operations. Much attention has been attracted by statistics that verify that owners of red cars submit more accident claims than owners of grey cars, with car insurers adjusting their premiums accordingly. Apply this colour-test approach to windows and the effect is noticeably similar. It's important to remember that most people, when they pass windows, are not thinking of shopping; their minds are elsewhere and it's quite a challenge to catch their eye and their imagination. Colour invariably does the job beautifully.

Because colour creates its own space and environment it demarcates its own parameters and creates a body of wholeness and containment, rendering it the perfect tool for windows which are themselves inherently compact. The vibrancy within that coloured space can do a lot of the work for you – much less propping is needed for example – but pitch of tone is crucial. A shade that's too sharp or slightly off can create an entirely different mood or story. The wrong blue, for instance, could be perceived as icy rather than serene which would be detrimental to say, a bathroom promotion. When I was choosing the yellow for my company Yellow Door, I wanted the tone to say 'positive', 'vibrant' and 'sunny', yet eggy yellow had something quite stodgy and bland about it, and lemon was too sharp. So, if you're using colour alone to tell the story in the window, the particular hue is pivotal. Quite often when I was working on windows and my team and I were brainstorming theme ideas, we found that expressing colour through tone was always the most difficult aspect. Each one has a character – grey, for example, is empiric, absorbing and reflects the colours that surround it. That's the flip side of working with something so versatile – the potential for error is greater.

But regardless of pitch of tone and the stories it can tell, colour unstintingly represents energy to me. It's so vital and omnipresent and luscious; it exudes *joie de vivre* – so intrinsically sensual and alive. Cosmetics houses, whose very business is built on the saleability of colours, appreciate the impact each shade has on the senses and exploit that essence, promoting seductive, fertile images of pouting lips, colour-dilated eyes and blushing cheeks in a seasonally rotating palette of hues. But colour can be bigger than the individual; it can also immediately signify country and season. Christina Kim, designer of the vibrant LA-based Dosa label, once remarked that when she went to India, she wasn't struck so much by the array of hot colours and Diana Vreeland's 'Pink is the navy-blue of India', as by the extraordinary number of different shades of white. The same could perhaps be said of black in the great metropolises of the Western World; there certainly seems to be an endless quest for the New Black.

It's fascinating that colour can hold so many different connotations for individuals and nations the world over, and yet also represent so many of the same. Like smell, it can conjure private memories, and yet colour's permanent association with certain qualities has seen it adopted by businesses who have made particular colours their own. Take Hermès' elegant orange or Tiffany's now-eponymous blue. Such powerful examples of colour-led packaging insist that, regardless of changes in the boardroom hierarchy, the company is not ephemeral or part of a trend. It is here – rooted, permanent, fixed. And the strength of association is such that colour and company can become synonymous, with people automatically equating orange with Hermès, and sky-blue with Tiffany.

One example of a business which successfully switched its signature colours is the Italian house Gucci. In 1996, the designer Tom Ford ousted Sloaney racing green and gold for dark slate-green and platinum. The house had completely repositioned itself on the international fashion scene and was aiming towards a more sophisticated, urban customer; but crucially Gucci retained the basic green it was known for and instead honed the new ideals of the company around a more severe black-based hue which symbolised minimalism, elegance and an industrial edge. This example of redefining a company through colour shows how powerful it can be in branding, as much in windows as on carrier bags and logo wrapping paper.

But for a colour to be an effective tool, it needn't be used alone. The repetition of colours can be just as strong and really bring home a mood if you work within a tight spectrum. I once executed a window in which a line of floorboards was propped against the wall and painted the symphony of yellows through to oranges, with matching-toned clothes hanging very simply in front. It was so vibrant and zesty, I used to stand in front of it, absorbing its warmth. It felt like a Mediterranean summer, and gave off its own light – attracting customers like moths to a flame.

'...colour elicits a physiological response, with the eye reacting most quickly to bold colours like orange, red and yellow...'

Above and following pages *This sequence of windows demonstrates the interaction between colour, light, mannequins and props. The windows reflect the retailer's very authoritative brand position in a whimsical, almost throwaway, manner.*
Gucci, New York

'...colour creates its own space and environment.'

Above *Given that Emporio Armani is the diffusion label for Giorgio Armani, this funky, accessible and cool window cleverly targets the younger customer who might not yet have considered the signature label for occasion wear. The metallic colours feel young and vibrant and lend an energy to the rather more restrained clothes.*
Emporio Armani, New York

Opposite *The simplicity of the colour tones is very striking here. The vivid red birds amongst the accessories have to work hard to be seen against the looming, shadowy backdrop, but their colour catches the eye, and therefore the attention, of passers-by.*
Saks Fifth Avenue, New York

Left *A wonderful display of baskets and other handmade items taps into the ethnic trend which influences every strand of culture, from fashion to interiors to sculpture and music. In the bazaar atmosphere of this window, the colours are discreet, tonal and understated, yet rich in array.* **Printemps, Paris**

Right *This story, a design by Paul Muller, is so ultra-feminine it's almost kitsch – it's the kind of candy-pink you see in 1950s Hollywood movies. Re-creating a dressing room in this colour and layering it with hats, sidelined in the modern wardrobe for special events only, extols the virtues of grooming and revives an old-fashioned glamour.* **Liberty, London**

HAT SALON
LIBERTY
GROUND FLOOR

BRAND-NEW STYLE

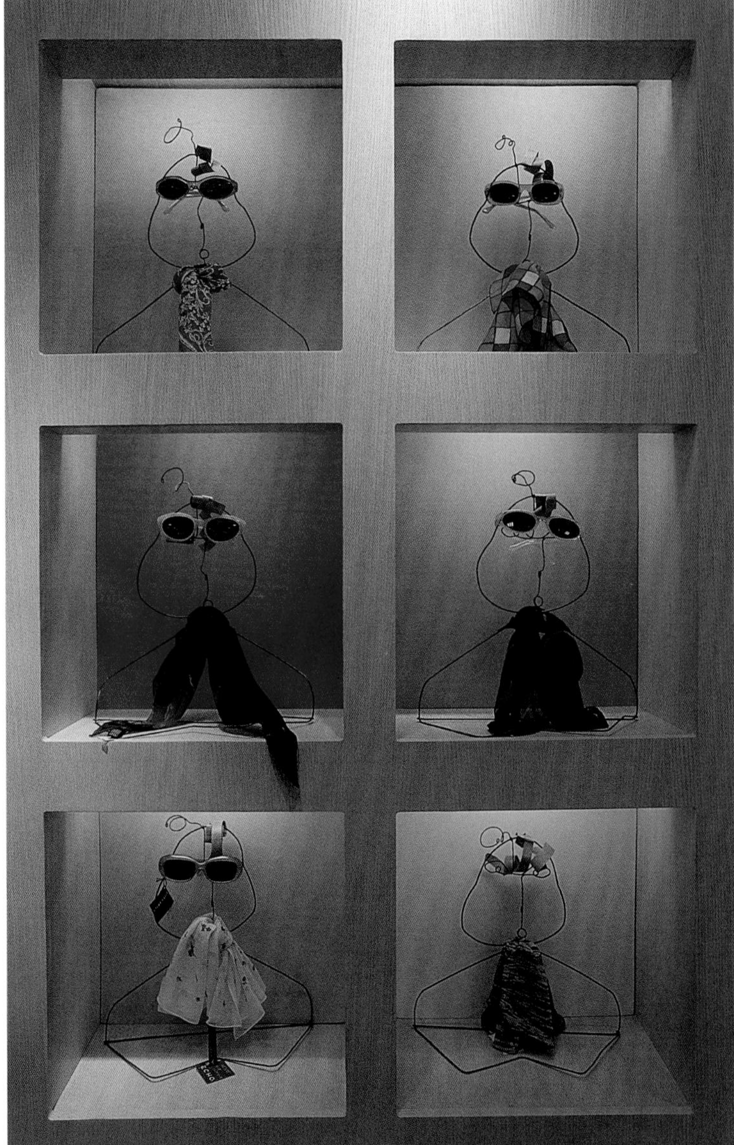

Above *The solid blocks of colour in this display are as controlled as the product grouping. They are contained within a strictly defined area, which serves to heighten the intensity of each block. Everything feels very precise and whole, without compromise.* **Bloomingdale's, Newport Beach**

Left *The ruthless symmetry of this window is softened by the scheme's sorbet colours. Cool blues are juxtaposed with butter-yellow, grass-green and brown while the products gently mirror the lines of the set's checks with shoes, shirts and ties all arranged neatly in a mathematical sequence.* **Matsuzakay, Japan**

Kochopt

Above *I love the way this swimwear – shown in the acid-bright colours immediately associated with mouth-watering chewy sweets – is displayed on transparent mannequins whose forms appear to be cast from water; suspending the models from the ceiling adds to this sense of buoyancy.* **Dickins & Jones, London**

Left *Big isn't necessarily beautiful, and scale doesn't need to be large to be bold. In this display, the eye is drawn to the bags precisely because they're so tiny, like little birds and nests in winter trees.* **Wako, Tokyo**

Opposite *The ultimate colour window. The depth of the colour, the texture and the 3-D effect work together in an utterly absorbing and calming display.* **Kochoptik, Zurich**

'Colour gives the world personality and depth.'

Top left *The holograms here play a double role. The flashing strobe colours hint at the technology of the sunglasses' lenses which no doubt filter ultraviolet light, and the rainbow-like colours make them feel organic and summery.* **Chanel, Zurich**

Above left *The sheer force of these citrus colours demands the viewer's attention. The bold, naive illustrations gradually pull the eye down to the sunglasses which appear to be offering shade from the glare. Stop-'em-dead displays don't come much more graphic than this.* **Diem Look Optik, Zurich**

Top right *These wonderful jellyfish props demonstrate perfectly how colours can interact with fabrics and surfaces. The translucency of the chiffon demands layering in order to build up a rich, opaque tone, but it also causes the colour to become three-dimensional.* **Ducan, Zurich**

Above *These contrasting colours – greens and blues played against pinks, yellows and oranges, with the backdrop echoing the sun – are warm, bright and happy: the perfect setting for showing off picnic wares.* **Galeries Lafayette, Paris**

Opposite *Primary colours are indelibly associated with children's toys and therefore with function and durability. These plastic watering-cans have been arranged into a cartoon pastiche, adding a touch of humour to a product that might otherwise have been difficult to remove from its functional purpose.* **Siebler, Zurich**

Following pages *Layers of dull reds, greens and yellows in this Christmas display create a deliberately manufactured jumble. The chaos is heightened by the strong, dark colours, which aren't relieved or brightened with much light; the window, suitably, feels very atmospheric and moody. The energy is as palpable as the colours are striking!* **Barneys, New York**

the
of
Soul
Barneys New York
would like to thank

ARETHA
YULE

Opposite *This display by Naomi Yamamoto is a great example of how to invest a festive scheme with energy and a modern slant without resorting to those tired staples, tinsel and glitz. The colour stories are hazy and muted; the lights are designed to resemble mistletoe; and the clean lines of the tree are spare and elegant.*
Shiseido, Japan

Seasons

Joyeux Noël

'It's easy for the new season's windows to look fresh because they come in immediately after the sale, but pace yourself. It's a designer's job to think in terms of an entire season, but windows should reflect what people want now, not two months down the line. Start gently with key colours and don't put the strongest pieces in immediately. Keep an element of surprise and spontaneity and go with the weather – bright summer colours look out of sync on a dark day. It's all about reading the mood of the street.' Joseph

The endless cycle of the seasons has long been a source of motivation in the artistic world, but although poets, painters and composers draw their inspiration from just four, in the course of a year, modern retailers have to account for no less than eight seasonal displays in their windows and a minimum of twelve ideas per season: January sales; the first spring statements; Easter; summer wardrobes; the summer sales; new autumn collections; winter looks; and, of course, the big one, Christmas. These are the foundations of retailing; accordingly retailers have consistently to create schemes that are individual and unique within these universal theme frames.

Christmas is, of course, the most important. In New York – where next year's festive scheme is planned the day after this year's has been installed – the Christmas windows are a celebration, much in the way that London regards its Christmas lights, which are sponsored by designers such as Yves Saint Laurent and endorsed by celebrity openings. The significance of Christmas windows is reflected in press coverage of the festive displays, which provides a great opportunity for astute retailers to stimulate public interest in their business and to benefit from some free advertising. Only the tiniest percentage of the consumer population doesn't buy into Christmas, so with the nation at large on a hunt for gifts and decorations, retailers certainly expect their sales to increase dramatically. But it should be acknowledged that potential customers are also being targeted by every other store on the block. Give energy and try to appeal to the customer – give them a reason to want something and a want to buy it.

I certainly wouldn't recommend telling the true story of Christmas through windows because altruism set in a commercial environment doesn't work. The window's motifs must correspond to the image and branding of your business, and few businesses, let alone retailers, have anything to do with the redemption and salvation of mankind! Rather, the one element in every Christmas window should be the upbeat element of fun – the essence of the Christmas spirit as opposed to the biblical representation itself, which so often resembles a shoddy pantomime or school-play naivety. Critics might say steering clear of the religious theme isn't the true face of Christmas, but I would counter that the true face of Christmas isn't about presents and selling. Whatever the season, the retailer's bottom line is sales – gifts and stocking-fillers during the Christmas period – and the intent is to sell merchandise under the Christmas guise of goodwill, so create a festive scheme that is polished, elegant and sparkling. My favourite Christmas window was one I executed for Harvey Nichols telling the story of Yule Tide and Mistle Toe. We created some huge fairy-tale cartoon sketches, with Yule Tide as the hero and Captain Crack Pot and his Crackers as the baddies. Three days before Christmas, so the story went, Yule Tide decided to check on Captain Crack Pot's factory which was making presents for all the children. When he arrived he saw that none of the presents had been made and all the money had been spent. As punishment Captain Crack Pot was banished to King Harrods's emporium and all the presents were bought at Harvey Nichols so that the children would have a wonderful Christmas after all. It was tremendously successful because it took literal elements of Christmas and spun an interpretation that was captivating, energetic and humorous. I don't know how much Harrods laughed!

To retailers, the 'bleak midwinter' means only one thing – January sales. Nothing diffuses the festive spirit faster than clearing the windows three or four days *before* Christmas. I understand the problem – the stylist doesn't want to come in on Boxing Day to strip it all for the January sale – but what a waste. If you've bombarded the public with Christmas spirit since early November, it's tactless, and shows bad taste, to take away the ambience for customers doing last-minute shopping in the immediate run-up to Christmas Day. This is the time when money is spent on bulk and emergency purchases; stripping away the festive veneer is a waste of an opportunity. I don't think people mind if the windows are cleared on the first day of the sale – there's always so much bustle and anxiety to get inside that the windows are relegated to the sidelines in the customer's mind. As long as the sale was preceded by marketing which communicated the sale and the store's image to the public, then people entering the store are probably already customers.

Many retailers are embarrassed by sales and try to get them over with as quickly as possible, which is a shame, I think, as customers enjoy them. They don't in any way undermine your brand as they are by definition simply the sale of leftover stock, not merchandise that is defective or cheap. Presentation is crucial to promoting this viewpoint. My real *bête-noire* is the 'pile-it-high' approach, with sale items just dumped in a heap. A sale is not an excuse to leave windows unstyled and merchandise shabby and shoddy. Keep the message sharp, focused and well presented. Psychology is a powerful tool in sales promotions. Red, for example, is uppermost in people's minds when they think of sales, so work with the power of that colour. Stop them with it. And give time to the stories you can depict with the merchandise – merchandise you were promoting at full price just a couple of months before. I did a sales promotion which showed estate agents' 'For Sale' signs and the boot of a car opened up for a 'car boot sale'. It was funny and light and diffused the 'cut-price' stigma. Bear in mind that the sale might be some of your customers' only opportunity to shop at your store, so make them feel as special as the last of the big spenders. They should see smart polished windows and receive good customer service; don't emblazon 'sale' all over your carrier bags – it doesn't make the customer feel good. Everybody loves a bargain, and there's a world of difference between a bargain and something cheap. Designing windows within the constructs of seasons can be difficult, but maintain an impetus for freshness and vigour and pride, and it will be as Shakespeare wrote: 'How many things by season season'd are/To their right praise and true perfection!'

'Give energy and try to appeal to the customer – give them a reason to want something and a want to buy it.'

Top *Half-human, half-beast mannequins model quiet clothes in a surreal landscape. A topiary Christmas tree is the only indicator of Christmas, with erratic and vividly hued lighting lending a dark edge to the scene. This is Christmas for grown-ups.* **Barneys, New York**

Above *The secular meets the divine in a postmodern interpretation of Christmas. What do they look like? What do they wear? With their assured, down-to-earth poses, it's clear that these angels won't fear to tread anywhere.* **Marshall Field's, Chicago**

Above *Feasting puts the festivity into Christmas. The products are gently caught in the light, with a Tiffany blue box catching the dim moonbeam above. Will Father Christmas deliver that dream present? Anything's possible in Never-Never Land. Well, almost anything...* **Tiffany & Co., London**

Opposite *The sheer drama of Christmas captured by Paul Muller in a cameo of hedonism – a portrait of success within excess, of celebrity within celebration.* **Liberty, London**

LIBERTY

MERR

Above *Christmas is nothing if not for children, and the myths, legends and rituals surrounding it perpetuate that charm. The vibrant candy colours and marzipan-like textures of this childlike sculpture of Pinocchio nourish the eye and feed the imagination.* **Seikatsu Soko, Japan**

Above Here, a rainbow-coloured cityscape is moulded from Plasticine to create the sense of movement, bustle and energy that characterizes city life. The motifs associated with a Victorian Christmas are present, but in an urban setting. **Mitsukoshi, Japan**

Following pages, left *This display by Peter Rank draws on the pagan myth of the green man whose floribundance in the bleakest month of the year represents fertility and new beginnings. There's tremendous majesty to this figure which has been brilliantly executed; the clean white lights and burnished gold stars add a touch of festive magic.* **Godasse, Munich**

Following pages, right *It's impossible to walk past the gleam of the gilt coming from this window, another design by Peter Rank. In contrast, the mannequin herself is starkly restrained, with her neat Louise Brooks bob, porcelain skin and tidy body language. Knowing when to hold back is half the trick.* **Fröhlich, Munich**

Above and opposite *Music brings goodwill and peace among men at Christmas. There's a sense of movement and gaiety in the woodwind players' legs and the rich medieval colours strike the right note. Products are placed just so, as incidentals, props even, keeping attention on the festivity of the occasion.* **O. C. Tanner, Salt Lake City**

poco rit.
a tempo
piu forte
dim. poco a poco
molto rit.
REJOICE
Fine

'...modern retailers have to account for no less than eight seasona

'isplays in their windows and a minimum of twelve ideas per season...'

Above and opposite *High camp and kitsch work well within the heightened drama of occasions such as Christmas, and these witty tableaux exploit both within the confines of a well-known carol.* **O. C. Tanner, Salt Lake City**

Above and opposite *Irreverent and witty, these peeks behind the curtains of famous personalities at Christmas prompt a smile from the passer-by. Good taste is not a prerequisite of a successful Christmas display, that's for sure.* ***Barneys, New York***

'The window's motifs must correspond to the image and branding of your business...'

Above *Eat, drink and be merry: I wouldn't mind an invitation to this Christmas party!* **Bergdorf Goodman, New York**

Opposite *A great window by Andrea Graham. An outsize Rastafarian's dreadlocks are lit by fairy lights so that he looks like both the Christmas tree and the fairy, but his casual clothes and 'at ease' stance are a break away from the glitz usually associated with Christmas.* **Daffy's, New York**

'A sale is not an excuse to leave windows unstyled and merchandise shabby and shoddy...'

Above *Window display meets Pop art as graphic shapes and colour-blocking assault the eye. Stop-'em-dead colours – red, yellow and black – pull no punches and the glass is used as the canvas for the display.* **Manor, Zurich**

'...Keep the message sharp, focused and well presented...'

Above *Half the man he used to be: a realistic mannequin is set on the floor in a comic interpretation of half-price merchandise. Quirky details like his hand and nose pressed to the glass imply both a sense of urgency – the sale ends soon – and challenges passers-by to take notice as he stares out at them.* **Anon, San Francisco**

Following pages *A very simple and yet a very effective display by Paul Muller. Crockery in the same brilliant yellow as the daffodils is placed in an industrial setting where it mirrors the brightness and cleanness of the flowers.* **Liberty, London**

FRÜHLINGS
22000.
Samt NERZ
14900.-

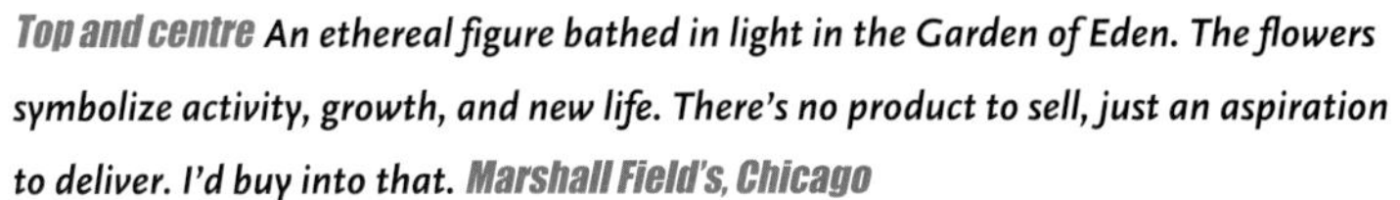

Top and centre *An ethereal figure bathed in light in the Garden of Eden. The flowers symbolize activity, growth, and new life. There's no product to sell, just an aspiration to deliver. I'd buy into that.* **Marshall Field's, Chicago**

Below *This window is selling a concept, not a product. A brilliantly coloured tropical bird flashes past the daring uniformity of backdrop, product and props in an affirmation of the arrival of spring.* **Central Park, Japan**

Opposite *The vibrancy of the green backdrop and the clever lighting of this display by Peter Rank reinforce the freshness, newness and fertility of spring, with hopping Easter bunnies adding a touch of humour.* **Fröhlich, Munich**

***Right** The clash of textures here – smooth stones, crackling twigs, a velvety backdrop – ensures that the eye has to search hard for the products which have been naturally absorbed into the scene.* **ZCMI, Salt Lake City**

Promotions

'The core elements of a promotional window display are the products and ancillary design elements – colour, proportion, texture and juxtaposition. It's like an editorial feature brought to life, drawing the potential customer directly into the world of the products displayed and the retail environment promoting them.'

Aerin Lauder, Director, Creative Product Development, Estée Lauder

Promotional windows are like marriages, dependent for success upon mutual respect, imagination and compromise. There should be a sympathy between the retailer and the promoter which allows each to flourish, yet often they descend into Faustian tragedy, one selling their soul to the other. It's a potentially tricky situation, two separate companies with distinct images dependent on each other for trade. The promoting company, for example, may be looking to run a promotional window in tandem with an advertising campaign, but that campaign may be at odds with the retailers' customers; it's a matter of finding common ground, and achieving a balance. Magazine fashion editors tackle the same dilemma, styling and interpreting the season's looks to appeal directly to the reader without pandering to designers and delivering 'advertorial'.

The basic premise for promotions is to understand, well before the issues of style and content of display are reached, exactly who your customers are and why they might want to buy into the promotion. Some windows can lead the public mood, providing a signpost for life and living – the changing seasons, fashion's new directions, innovations in homewares. Promotional displays are the detail-specific markers of these influences, showing the small print, selling the minutiae within the big picture. Unlike seasonal displays, they are product-specific and their intent is to create direct sales from the window; one way of furthering this aim is to continue the promotion in-store. Very often windows are like make-up, a slick of commercial promise that's only skin-deep; carry the promotion throughout the store and you'll reinforce the message that this is a product in which it's worth investing.

This product loyalty is conditional upon the host store branding the promotion in its image. Unless your store has an exclusive agreement, the same product may be on sale a block away, targeting the same sort of customer that you're seeking. At Harvey Nichols, for instance, the windows are scheme-specific and customers tend to live in the southwest London area. Harrods, on the other hand, a mere hundred yards away, instals stock-specific windows to appeal to the coachloads of tourists and visitors to London who visit the world-famous store in which you can buy anything in the world that is for sale. The two stores' merchandise is the same, and their customers invariably wealthy, but London is big enough for both: by placing emphasis on different details, each can appeal to a different customer.

A promotion doesn't need to be about big statements – there's no need to hit the customer over the head with it. Subtlety is important; one element of the advertising campaign might be adopted, perhaps a prop, a signature or a colour, rather than the full marketing arsenal. The intellect and self-determination of the customer, who in this age of computers, TV, videos and advertising is wise to marketing ploys and bombarded with too much information, will be flattered. Turning down the volume of a pitch still pays when the visuals are punchy: the more you know the less you need to show.

Promotions aren't confined exclusively to commercial launches. Seasonal promotions are rapidly entrenching themselves in the retail calendar as fixed opportunities, with stores exploiting St Valentine's Day, Mother's Day and Father's Day. Hallowe'en, virtually a national holiday in America, has broken free of its joke shop associations and is now gaining popularity in Europe too. Such promotions call for an entirely different approach as displays are not confined to a specific brand but to a generic event that falls outside the seasonally- and religiously-determined retail calendar. (However, it's not good to see a pumpkin plonked in a window at Hallowe'en without any relevance to the product: I witnessed an up-market lingerie shop do just that, and the effect was depressing rather than amusing.) The store may not be working within the parameters of a set brand's marketing offensive, but it does still work within a set scheme; rather like Christmas and Easter, the display team have to put a new spin on a consistent, annual theme, fulfilling certain criteria.

Seasonal promotions, like their tactical commercial cousins, boast an etiquette all of their own; keeping a display beyond its sell-by date for the sake of budgets or regimented time-allocation in the windows is to be avoided. There's nothing worse than seeing, say, a St Valentine's Day promotion on 20 February. Clearly, you haven't been able to sell your chocolate or lingerie. It's absolutely vital that the stock is removed immediately – nobody's interested in yesterday's news. It's important to pitch promotional schemes at the right time and know when to pull out, because ultimately customers, like time and tide, wait for no man.

Left *Home is where the hearth is! The grandeur of the architectural sketches is balanced by some homely touches of comfort – a reading light, a flower bowl, a padded chair.* **ZCMI, Salt Lake City**

Above *At the centre of chaos is calm. A relaxed, suited figure stands next to a furious, schizophrenic tower of hangers with shirts tucked randomly amongst the jumble.* **Barneys, New York**

Above *Using a clever anachronistic reference to the history of fashion, this display uses butterfly bows and an Edwardian crinoline to promote belts.* **Bloomingdale's, New York**

Father's Day Ju

Left *The flat, cartoon-like cut-outs set the 3-D products in relief. The muted tones and uniformity of line of the backdrop make the beautiful accessories stand out: plenty of ideas for smartening up dad!* **ZCMI, Salt Lake City**

Following pages, left *The traditional door-to-door salesman proffers trays and boxes of assorted wares with a reassuring authority that leaves the customer only to decide 'which?'* **Daffy's, New York**

Following pages, right *Cool blue lighting and geometric shapes reinforce the urbanity of the business suit. Tapered silhouettes create strong lines and lend an air of assurance, while the mirrored head-pieces allow the onlooker to picture himself wearing the product.* **ZCMI, Salt Lake City**

FFY'S

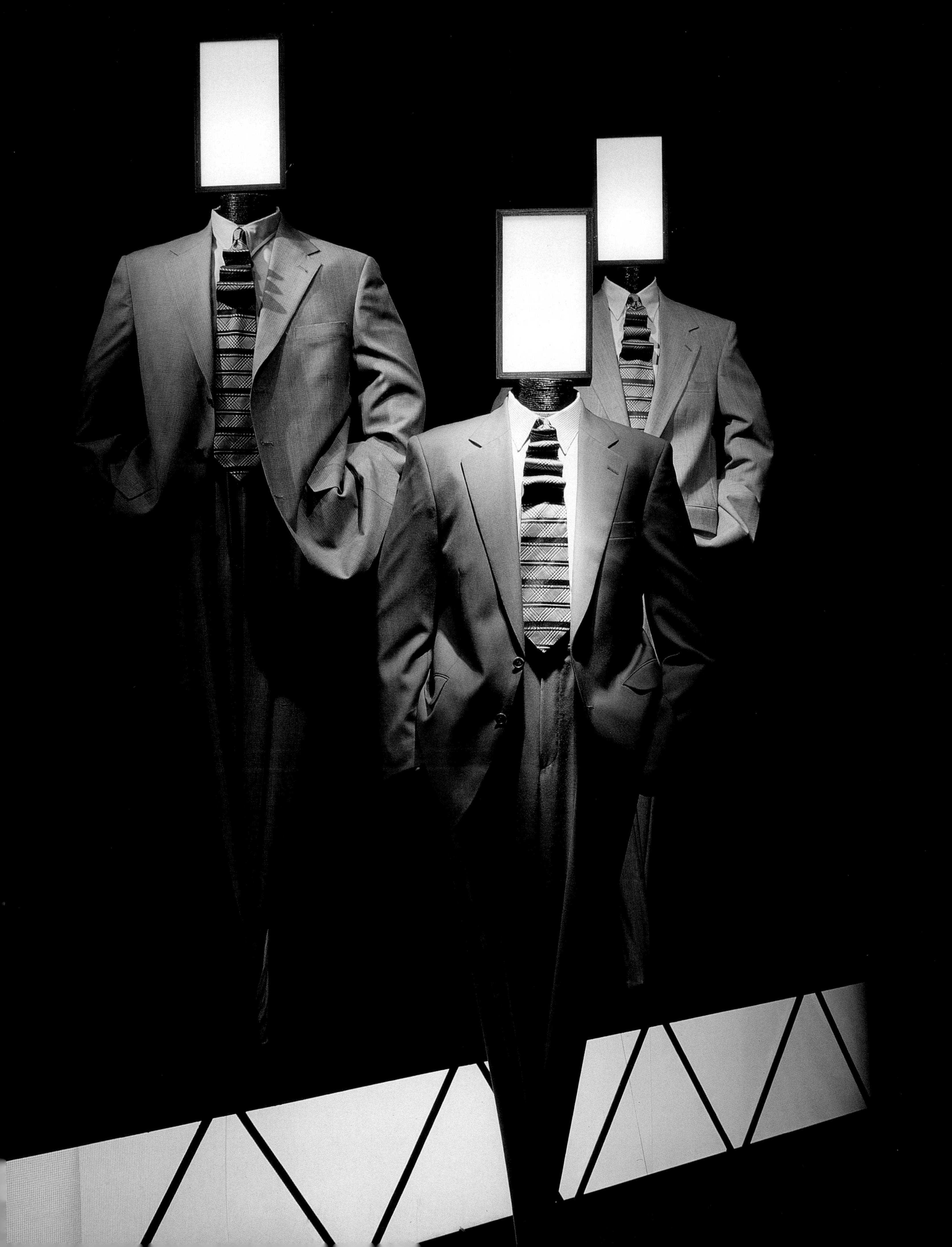

Above and opposite *Love across the divide – of the generation gap. Two images of romance: a passionate burst of graffiti, a universal art form that recognizes no distinctions of age, race or class, contrasted with a heart made of two halves, love's symbolic union, palely lit, dewy and pure.* **Tiffany & Co., London**

Top Shopping is a spectator sport. A line-up of footballers huddle on the bench, looking into the store as though watching a match. The grouping suggests team spirit and the lighting a dynamic, intense mood: shopping has replaced sport as the national pastime! **Carson Pirie Scott & Co., Chicago**

Centre The pecking order as never visualized before. In Chris Perry's 'costume meets cartoon' mural, naive story-book creatures in paradise colours scavenge for treasures from the jewelry department. **Harvey Nichols, London**

Below Brightly coloured drawers open to reveal hidden treasures to the delight of cartoon characters, whose excitement attracts the attention of passers-by. **Daffy's, New York**

Opposite The combination of Michelangelo's David and surfer's baggies reveals a great relationship between the store and the promoting company. Levi's have incorporated the style of their advertising campaign into the parameters of Bergdorf Goodman's image – witty, grand and modern. **Bergdorf Goodman, New York**

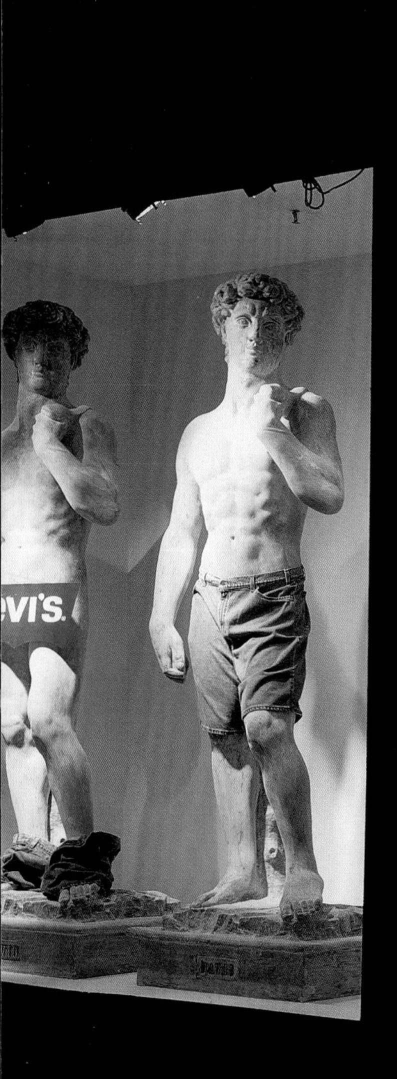

'A promotion doesn't need to be about big statements...the more you know the less you need to show.'

'Windows can lead the public mood, providing a signpost for life and living

the changing seasons, fashion's new directions, innovations in homewares.'

Above *Precariously balanced crockery blends with the chefs' hats, echoing the legend spelt out on the window.* **Barneys, New York**

Opposite *The stuff of champions. Products are placed on a podium in ascending order and presided over by a Hellenic figure.* **Anon, Paris**

TIFFANY & CO.
TIFFANY & CO.
TIFFANY & CO.
TIFFANY & CO.
TIFFANY & CO.

Left *A prime example of the games that can be played with light. By directing a bolder spotlight onto random areas of the prop, the passer-by is forced to hunt for the product, creating an interaction which is rewarded with surprise.* **Tiffany & Co., London**

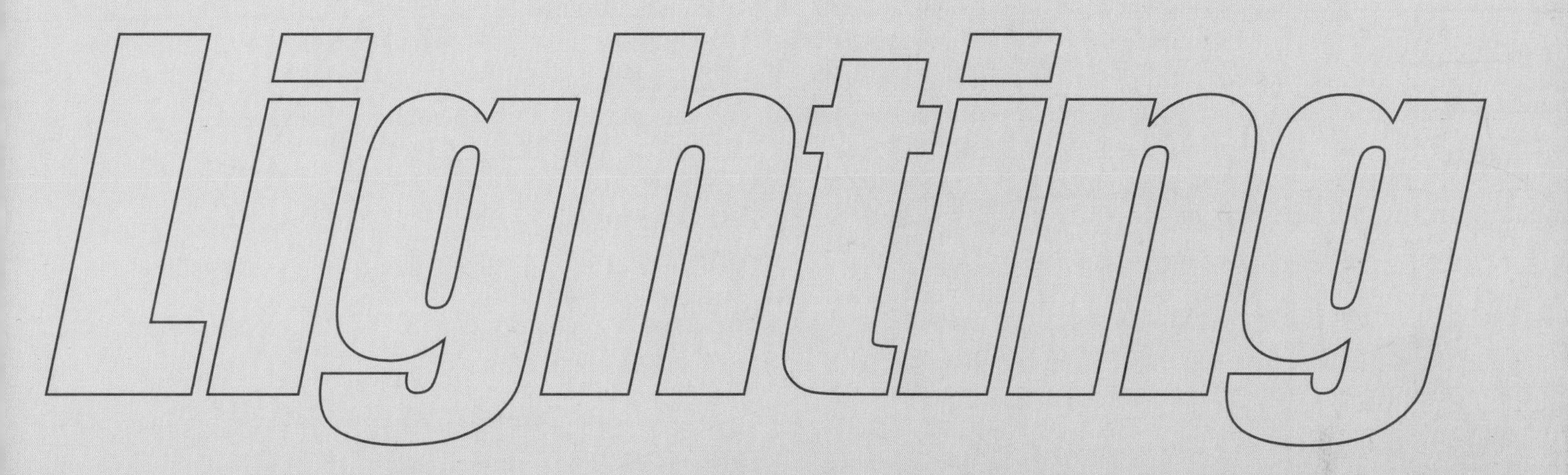

'Sophistication now is how to live and take care of yourself. It's about how, in the mad rush of things, we can find quality in our lives. Personal interpretation of light sets the mood for that. Light a room with twenty candles and it's the most beautiful thing.'

Arnold Chan, Isometrix

'And there was light.' The one element that literally switched on Creation and said the world was ready for business. The closed-set forum of the shop window lends itself very well to light's different volumes, intensities and dramas. Artificial light is not all-enveloping; it can only be perceived against darkness: just as the full moon only shines its luminous glory after sunset, so the spotlight depends upon an enveloping blackness for its pinpoint intensity. But if the sky's the limit for imagination – and maybe even budgets – there remain technical constraints. Daylight is much stronger than artificial light, so the aspect of the shop-front on the street in relation to the sky is quite important. On sunny days, for instance, you can't see into the windows, they look like black holes, so the trick is to use blinds – these act as a shield and set the windows in shadow, thereby making the artificial light much brighter. The reverse applies at night: if the window lights are too bright when it's dark outside they tend to bleach out the colours and fabrics in the space, so dimming them can redress the balance. It's a matter of intensity, and, you could say, of etiquette. It's not polite to submit customers to glare nor to force them to squint. Whatever mood the lighting is intended to arouse – through colour, spotlighting, movement, and so on – the wattage should attempt to re-create a natural light that feels neither garish nor dull.

The impact of light, the ultimate exponent of the visual experience, should never be underestimated. The shopping environment is a tightly controlled arena which launches an assault, on a subconscious level, on the customer's senses – from choices of music and background noise levels, to merchandising which encourages touch, and even the use of aroma. Traditionally, lighting's function in retail has been to highlight fabric quality and colour, especially in the winter months when the colour palette extends no further than black or grey. But windows – like any other marketing medium – are subject to fashion's caprices, such as the changes instigated by directional fashion houses such as Gucci and Prada. Prada likes to shine a flat light onto its clothes that gives a silhouette and traces a form. This is because what Prada is marketing is not the quality of the fabrics but a shape. A Prada window will typically feature a lit screen with just one flat hanging piece of clothing, or a bag or a shoe. They continue the philosophy in-store, with tables lit from beneath beaming up a silhouette, and clothes hanging in wall niches lit from above with an even, fluorescent light. The simplicity of this approach bears out the truth that a Prada shop requires minimal maintenance, proof once more that effect needn't come at great expense.

Armani takes a different approach. He was one of the first designers to re-create the home in his stores. They're not designed as huge architectural spaces but as comfortable little rooms, with upholstered furniture and table lamps. The home's cosiness and intimacy is re-created through localized light. Standard 100-watt ceiling light bulbs are banished; instead four 25-watt lamps are dotted at different heights around the room, fracturing the light across the space to create dispersing shadows and more visual interest. But while the home-style invites the shopper to relax, the windows are sharper and more concerned with an aesthetic signature. Armani single-handedly redefined the way women dress, putting them in softly-tailored, mannish suits and flat shoes; to reinforce the image upon which the label is based, the windows are specifically lit from both the top and bottom to eliminate shadow and to create clean and very flat images. Armani doesn't use mannequins as such but hangs a coat or dress, fully merchandised and lit from both directions, to create a very graphic representation of the shape.

Now, here's a dilemma. The most flattering light – the light in which women especially feel most comfortable – is a warm incandescent yellow that mimics candlelight. But the light that's most articulate for fabrics is a very cool, high-colour-rendering light. The two are opposites, and mutually incompatible; they create a catch-22 situation – flatter the customer into feeling good about herself, or flatter the designer's handiwork? The solution, and it isn't an easy one, is to mix the lights, 'saturating the spectrum' by merging warm into cool. Through precise positioning it's possible to bounce lights off various surfaces so that articulate lighting hovers over racks, rails and shelves, but a warmer light glows at the mirrors and in changing rooms. In retail, flattery will get you everywhere.

This dilemma highlights the importance of having variety and flexibility in light positions – ceiling lights, footlights and side rails – which allow you to choreograph a mood. Two inches can be all it takes: footlights shining in front of a voile, for instance, render it opaque and yet if lights are instead positioned directly behind, such a voile would become transparent. Uplighting creates an unsettling ghostly effect, whilst the light people feel most comfortable with comes from above, a subconscious echo of the sun. Like photosynthesizing plants, the human body and mind are nurtured by light, and especially sunlight. Therapeutic aspects of light are being adapted for the consumer, most commonly in conjunction with colour. Ian Schrager's new St Martin's Lane Hotel in London boasts chameleon light-boxes that saturate rooms in rainbow colours, whilst Philip Starck's Los Angeles hotel, the Mondrian, has illuminated bedheads that light up the whole of the bed frame, alternately soothing or energizing according to whim.

Aside from its psychological benefits and its arresting impact on the pedestrian, colour in lighting is also being hailed by the design world as the way to bring minimalism (the over-riding design influence of this century) forward. Gucci has positioned velvet, tuxedo-clad mannequins next to simple, brilliant neon-blue fluorescent tubes, and Prada has focused on coloured light bulbs, drenching window schemes in lilac, fuschia and pistachio hues. But it's not just about pretty colours. In order to stop pedestrians and seduce them into shopping, window design has to be a sophisticated marketing medium, a three-dimensional event as engaging as the theatre or a Sony Playstation. It has to be organic, an animated stage that uses colour and movement and drama to achieve an ambience with energy and image. Quite literally, window design is about painting with light.

'The closed-set forum of the shop window lends itself very well

to light's different volumes, intensities and dramas.'

Opposite *Here golden lighting has been slanted to imitate sunlight, immediately setting the scene out of doors. The pile of pasta in the corner, which looks like wheat, continues the wholesome and whimsical theme.* **Barneys, New York**

Above *The colder tones and intense shadowing of this neighbouring display convey a darker, more threatening mood; this is supported by the model's tense pose as she shies away from huge, attacking bugs.* **Barneys, New York**

Following pages, left *The bounty of the seas: golden trinkets from the deep are washed up on a rocky shore in a window which exploits the contrast between textures.* **Anon**

Following pages, right *Hidden treasures of the deep: in this window the precious pearl necklace is twined around a sculptural piece of coral, and surrounded by a starfish halo which draws the eye to the centre of the composition.* **Tiffany, Zurich**

189.–
209.–

***Above and opposite** By re-creating the rippled reflections in water, this display is at once restful and yet gently stirring. The potency of the deep blue and the white light in the water enhance the gleaming appeal of the product.* **Anon**

Following pages, left *The subtlety of the joke and the absurdity of treating fragile light bulbs as golf balls creates a witty display: light can be used for more than just illumination!* **Bergdorf Goodman, New York**

Following pages, right *Fluorescent tubing styled into graphic spaghetti hair feels young, funky and vibrant in a window best suited to a night-time audience.* **Anon, Düsseldorf**

SPORTS
ON 3

Left *Universally recognized landmarks can be given an amusing twist to attract passers-by. The projected flag suggests movement, whilst the brighter light on Barbie and her presidential pals at Mount Rushmore casts the lone figure on the drum podium in the foreground in slight shadow.* **FAO Schwarz, Boston**

Right *By positioning the sequinned backdrop – another Pop art icon – in the shade, glamour is attached to the product in the limelight by association. The necklace glistens but the eye is still drawn back to Monroe's unforgettable face. But then, that's star quality for you.* **Tiffany & Co., London**

Opposite *The necklace is bathed in a pool of intense light, highlighting its preciousness, while a clean, bright spot casts distinct shadows over a little wooden artist's mannequin in a miniaturized and self-referential shop window display.* **Tiffany & Co., London**

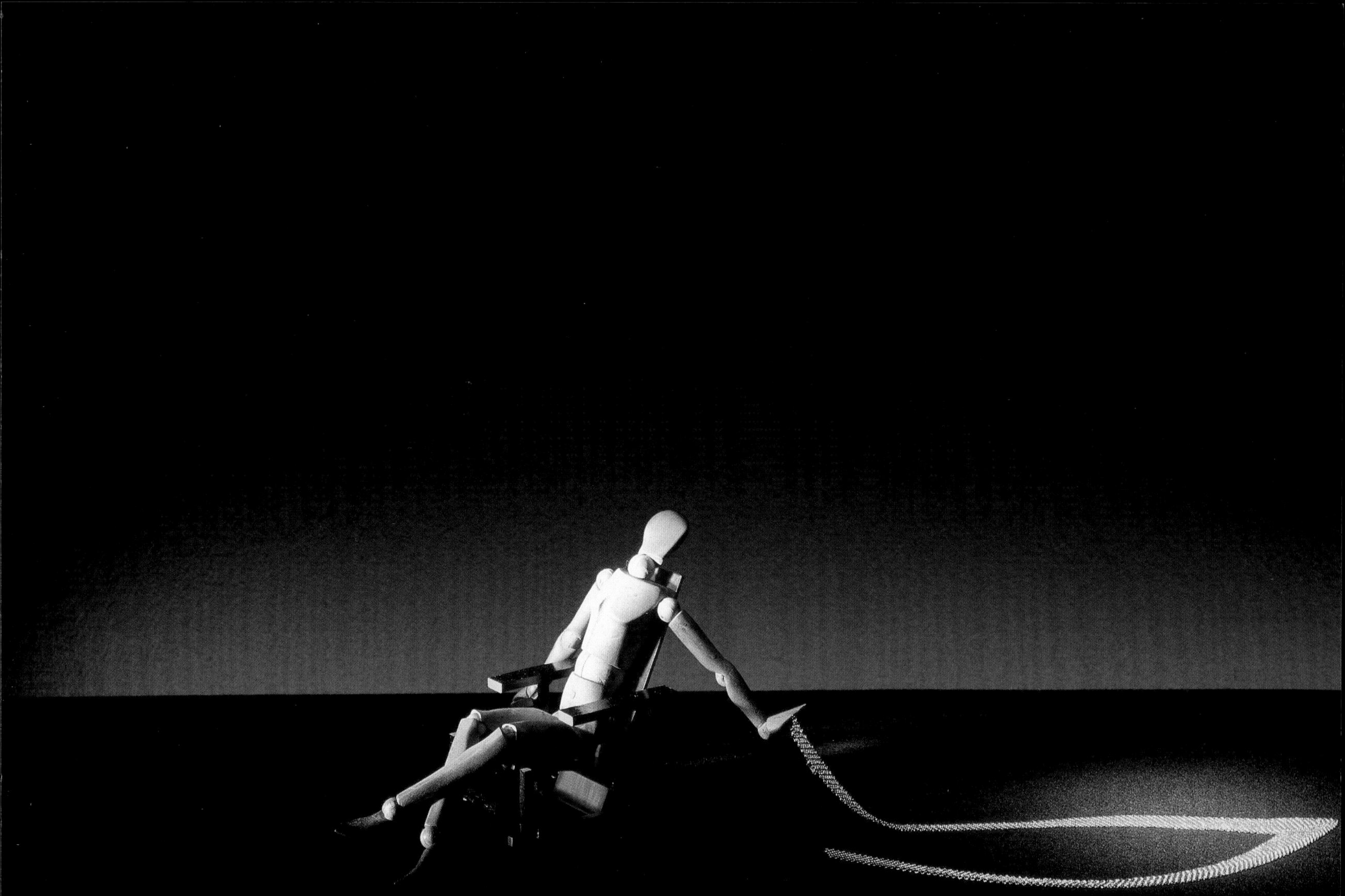

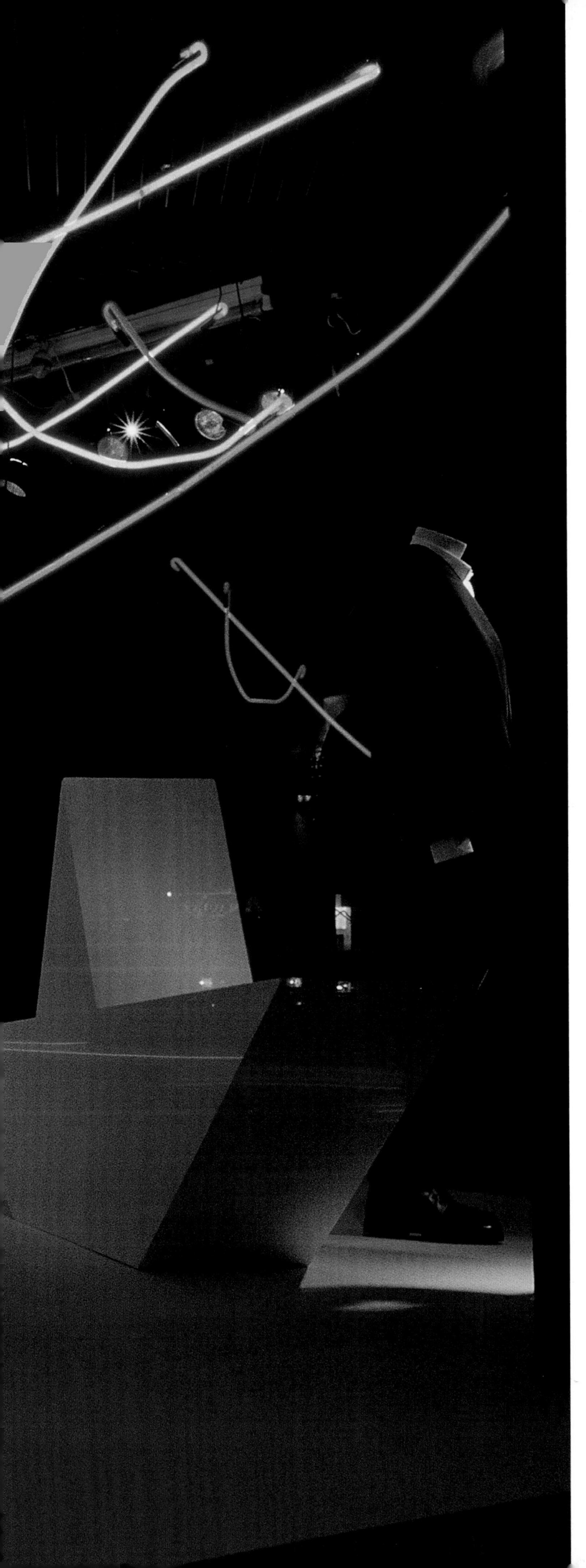

Left *Frozen as in time-lapse photography, the energetic trajectories traced by these neon tubes are full of movement and energy, in contrast to the calm, informal pose of the mannequins. The eye is drawn to, and held by, the constantly changing light patterns.* **Saks Fifth Avenue, New York**

Following pages *Colour-saturated light hits the mannequins and the coil-patterned backdrop with soft purpose. The low light density creates a cool atmosphere that feels at once modern and urban.* **Saks Fifth Avenue, New York**

DIANE VON
ON 7

Opposite *This window has been styled to look unstyled: the jumble of a fish market; the mannequins caught mid-movement; and the figure wearing an animal mask adding a touch of surreal humour to the scene.* **Bernie's, Zurich**

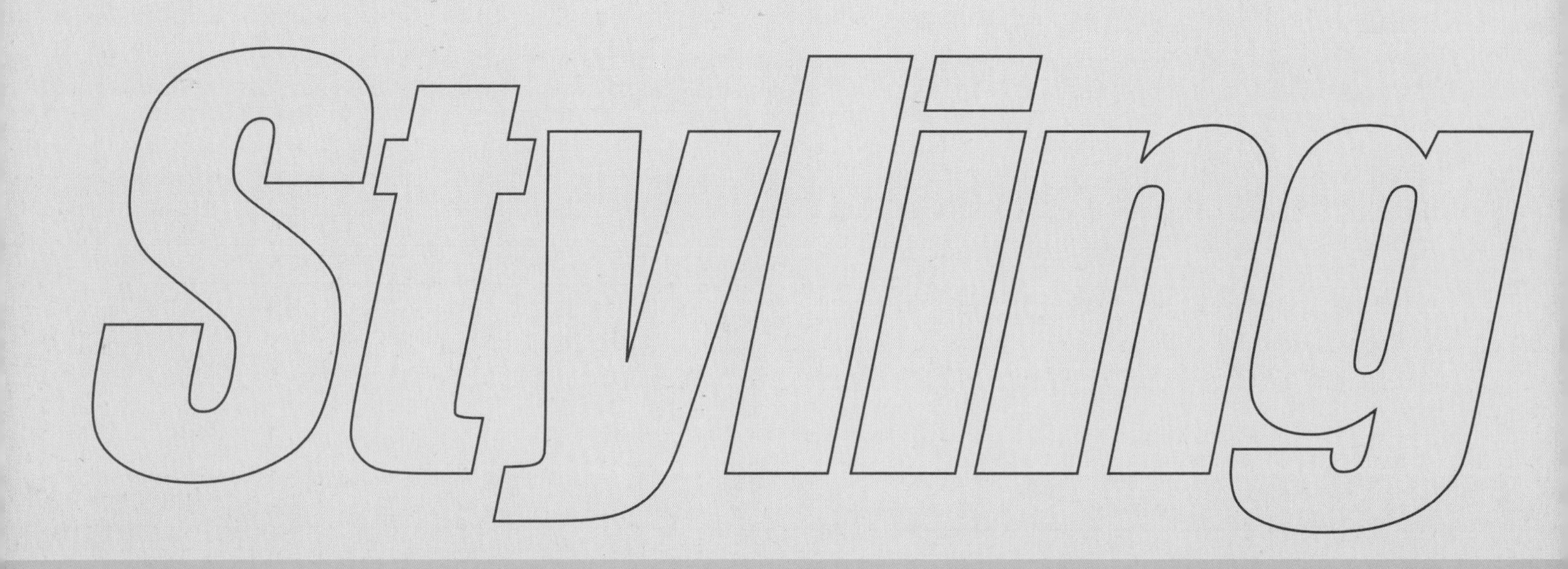

Styling

DIESEL
FUNGHI DEI PRATI
DIESEL
L'Amante
CHARLES CHEVIGNON

‘I don’t mind bad taste. No taste is what I’m against.’ Diana Vreeland

Taste, surely one of the most powerful and elusive forces in the late 20th century, and something impossible to define, describe or teach, holds a vice-like grip on today’s society in which supermodels mix with leaders of nations, and magazine editors, not politicians, represent the common voice. As many aspects of today’s world, from communities to technology, get smaller, status is increasingly invested in the details and the small print. Two of the greatest exponents of contemporary style – Tom Ford of Gucci and the supermodel Kate Moss – admit that the secret of modern taste lies in skilful editing. Ford is famous for paring his collections down to just the must-have skirt/trousers/shirt combination, and Moss reportedly won’t leave home before removing one element from her outfit, be it a necklace, a jacket or a hairpin.

But edited or not, the way Kate Moss wears an outfit will be completely different from the way the same outfit is worn by the average girl on the street. Moss’s job is to know about the details that count – maybe she just has an ‘eye’ for what works. I think the same applies to window stylists. Many people think that the styling of a window can be left to a sales assistant, but although styling a window – like getting dressed – is something anyone can do, it’s very hard to teach people taste and a sense of the scale they’re working to; as a result the inexperienced often go completely the wrong way, and, rather than editing, they tend to overstyle, equating ‘strange’ with ‘different’.

Window display is most commonly compared with magazine features. But whereas a picture in a magazine is necessarily flat, a window is three-dimensional and seen in the round. Although in a magazine the stylist may be able to clip a dress at the back, the window stylist has to pin a dress so that it doesn’t look as though it’s been pinned. And you need a much hotter iron in window display! In a magazine, people flick through the pages quickly and imperfections can be airbrushed out of photographs before printing, but when people are staring through $\frac{1}{4}$-inch plate-glass, every crease will be noticed. No, to my mind, window display is much nearer to the fashion show. Both are concerned with an overall image; both require a built set; and, in each, lighting, hair, make-up and accessories play an important part. You’ve got to create an atmosphere, build a brand and sell a product – none of which is as easy as it looks.

One certain rule is that the more clothes you put on a mannequin the better it looks. But it’s a mistake to pile on too many clothes. If you’re doing a swimwear promotion, you’ve got to be quite innovative to get away with it, because what you’re actually doing is exposing masses of plastic flesh. And in, say, a daywear promotion, the stockings have to be the right denier and colour and the shoes the right height. Ask yourself whether the mannequin could walk out of the window in what it’s wearing – a belt wrapped around the neck or a coat hanging off one shoulder and trailing along the ground is kitsch, not clever.

Another rule is that it’s vital to inject a sense of movement into clothes in a window. A heavy coat over a big skirt just looks like a great big mass of fabric. In a fashion spread, the photographer would have the model walking along a road to give the clothes some sway;

the window stylist has to try to achieve the same effect by 'blowing' the skirt.

But if the sense of movement is limited and highly stylized, one variable that you can really have fun with is intensity. The pigment in a red dress is magnified tenfold if lit by red light; and lighting a black garment in blue or red gives it a luxurious feeling, an important point, this, because a black garment's quality is the most difficult to show off in a window. A cheap black will always look cheap, and very few blacks are the same. Try to work with a broad colour range: black will always sell, so if the store buyers have gone for any other colour schemes, jump on those instead. A wise buyer will have bought some 'feathers' – token, avant-garde pieces for the windows that don't have to recoup their costs – to spell out the identity of the store and give its brand an edge.

One thing a window display does have in common with a fashion-magazine shoot is that they're both about creating a fantasy. The viewers of both don't want to see themselves reflected back – they expect a larger-than-life, enigmatic aspiration. This can mean taking a look to extremes: when Azzedine Alaïa's figure-hugging designs were to the fore, the windows at Joseph displayed minute, size-6 dresses stretched onto the mannequins to accentuate the impression of clothing as a second skin. Equally, when you want to place emphasis on luxury, using garments a couple of sizes too big always works: nothing looks better than a size-14 sheepskin coat on a small model – it really fosters an image of being enveloped and swaddled in the clothes. And I always say that the jewelry houses should have special display copies made in glass and paste, because a diamond solitaire just won't sparkle for someone 15 yards away. Either go for really large fakes in bold sizes, or use plenty of smaller styles together – why stop at one necklace when you can have ten? This quantity over quality trick also works very well with a product that isn't being sold on its obvious aesthetic appeal. Hundreds of tennis balls, for example, will have much more impact than a solitary stray ball rolled into the middle of a set.

But perhaps the most important element is basic housekeeping. The carefully contrived illusion of a minimalist window – white floors, ceilings and walls – will be destroyed entirely if the mannequin is scratched, the paint is chipped or the glass is grubby. And just as a £2,000 dress would look cheap if its wearer hadn't bothered to wash or style her hair, so that dress in the window can't be expected to reflect its worth if there is fluff on the floor. Stores are cleaned every night after closing and that cleaning should include the windows.

These invariable rules are the basics of styling a window. Ultimately fashions and style don't change that much – the accessories set the tone and suggest contemporary taste. Jil Sander may set off a pencil skirt and shirt with flat shoes, no make-up and straight hair, but that same look is instantly redolent of the 1940s if styled with red lips, Mary Janes and a quiff. My favourite window has to be a St Valentine's Day display from the 1950s which showed a mannequin in a curvy Dior suit drilling through a concrete heart with a pneumatic drill. The same could be done today, because although fashions come and go, when you've got taste, style endures.

Above and opposite *The more clothes you put on a mannequin the better it looks: here the clothes are almost sculpted – with tubular wired hems and pleated square shoulders – as if to compete with the naked forms next to them.* ***Ka De We, Berlin***

'...You've got to create an atmosphere, build a brand and sell a product...

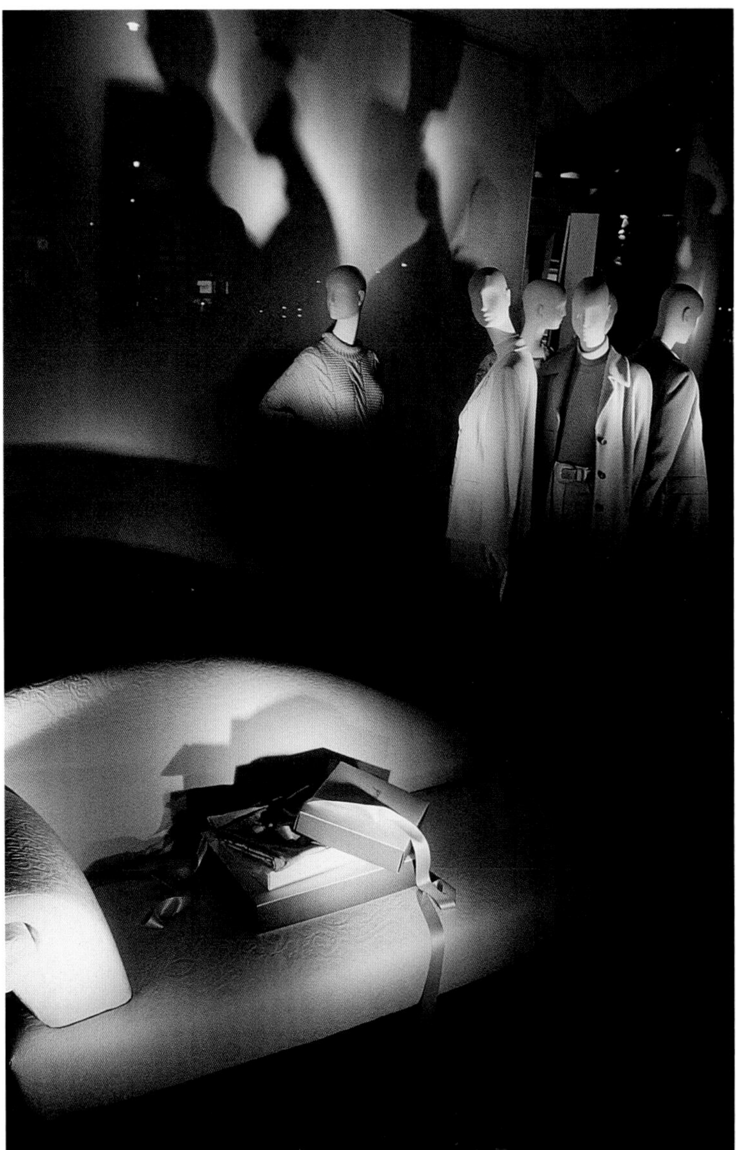

Opposite *The body language of the standing figure is so authoritative that words are unnecessary. The chairs and the shadows on the wall add to the sense of chaos and action, but they don't detract from the interaction between the two figures.* **Barneys, New York**

Above *This display shows chic, beautiful and understated garments against a backdrop of fashion sketches, their blueprints, as it were.* **Barneys, New York**

Above *You don't have to fill 20ft of window space just because it's available. Atmosphere and image create their own space, so play with sophisticated colour palettes, moody lighting and subtle suggestion, as here.* **Feldpausch, Zurich**

Above *The simplicity of this concept is as breathtaking as its intricacy. A seamless whole is achieved through careful pinning, while the lighting lends an ethereal mood. Although there's minimal content to this window – the products are the props – it's a deceptively high-maintenance display which relies on spotless housekeeping.*
Barneys, New York

Above *The scope of styles and colours available in this collection by Isobel Toledo is offset neatly, and humorously, by the lampshade heads painted by her husband Ruben Toledo. The heads' uniformity is made all the more striking by the variety of individual looks on offer.* **Barneys, New York**

Hosiery

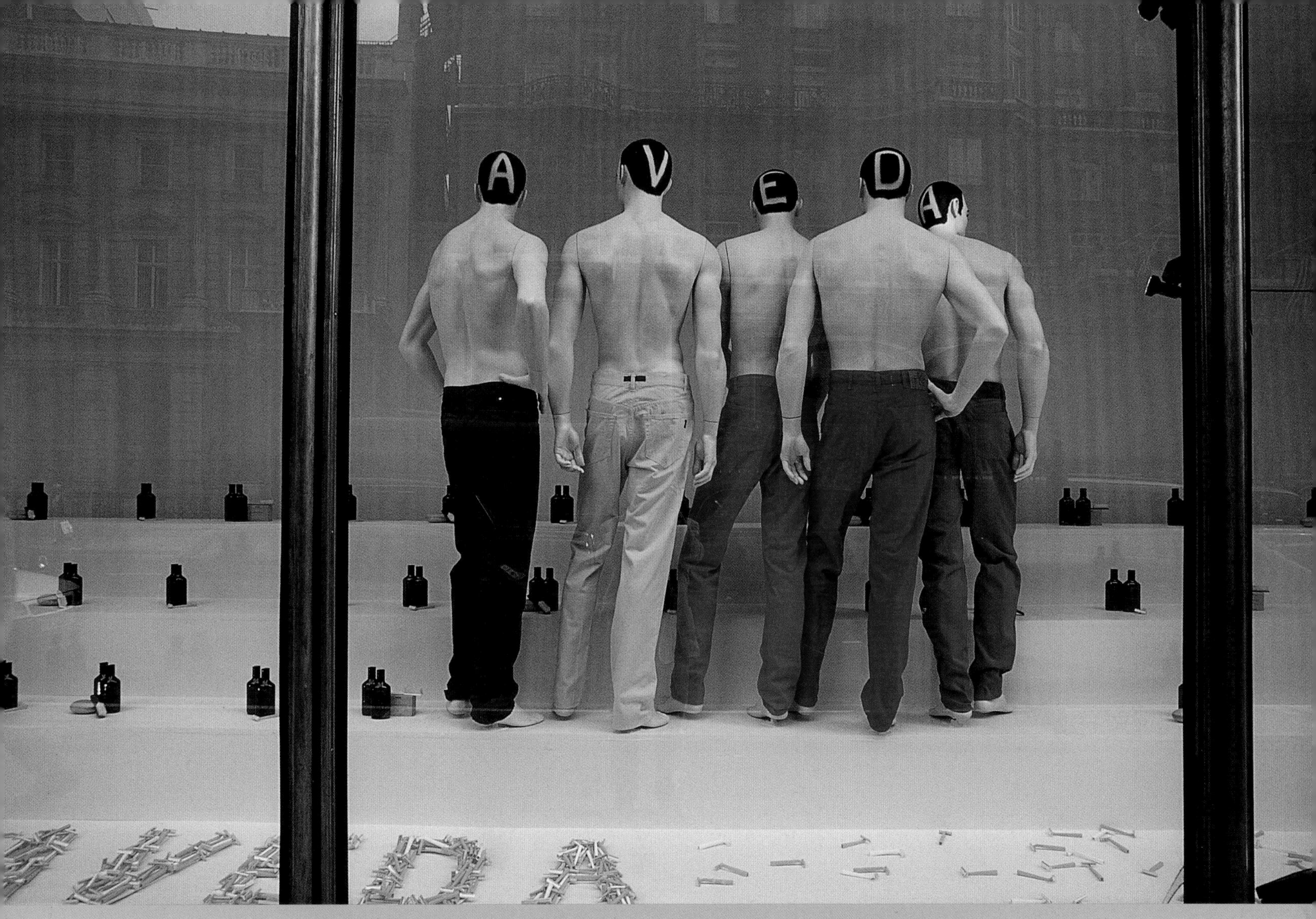

'...they're about creating a fantasy...'

Above Creating a buzz about a product is usually left to advertisements and other marketing devices, but this window takes the matter into its own hands. A cluster of mannequins, carefully grouped with their backs to the window, encourages passers-by to find out what is attracting so much attention. **Harvey Nichols, London**

Opposite Chris Perry's Lucy the Caterpillar became a London tourist attraction with her numerous hosiery-clad legs. She's certainly a show-stopper, guaranteed to halt shoppers in their tracks, but the display contains a commercial message too, making the product a necessary component of the prop. **Harvey Nichols, London**

'...it's very hard to teach people taste and a sense of the scale they're working to...'

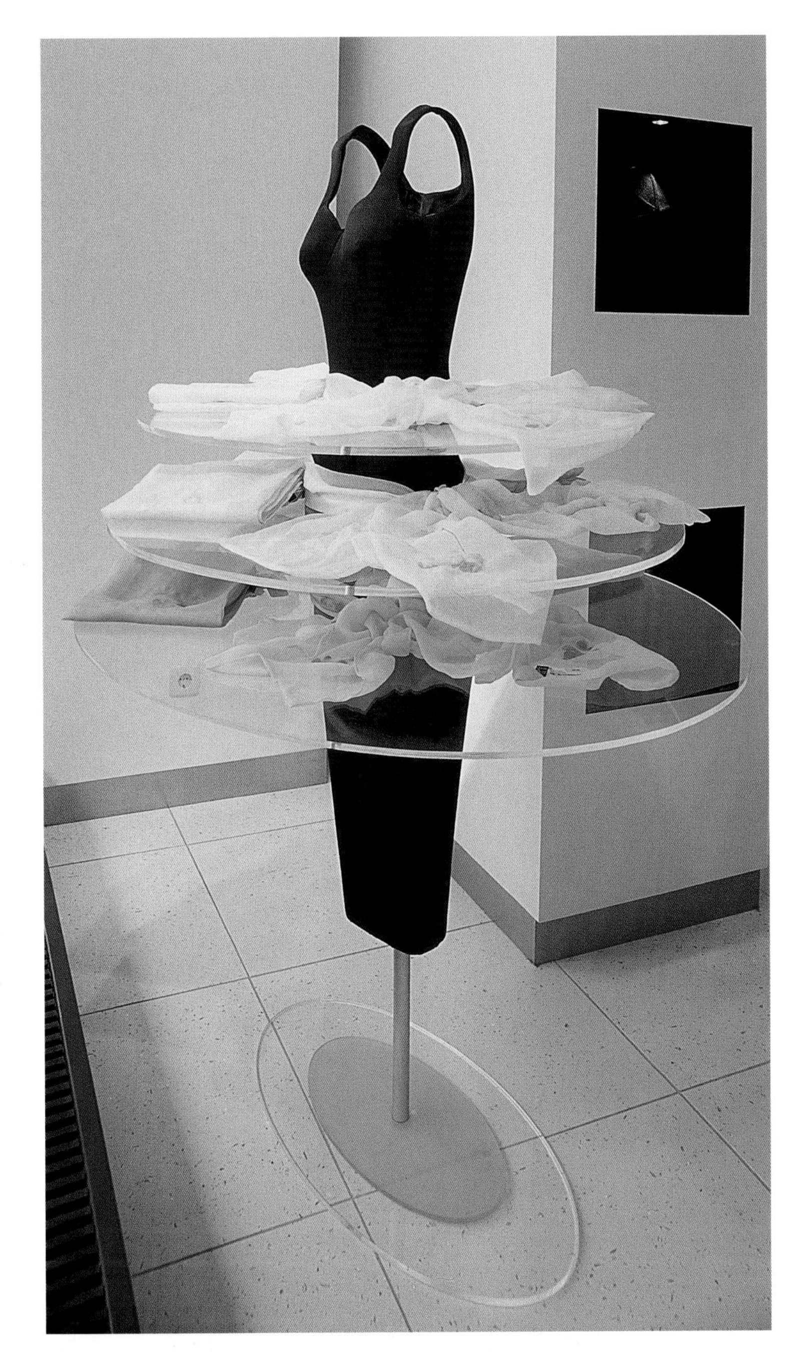

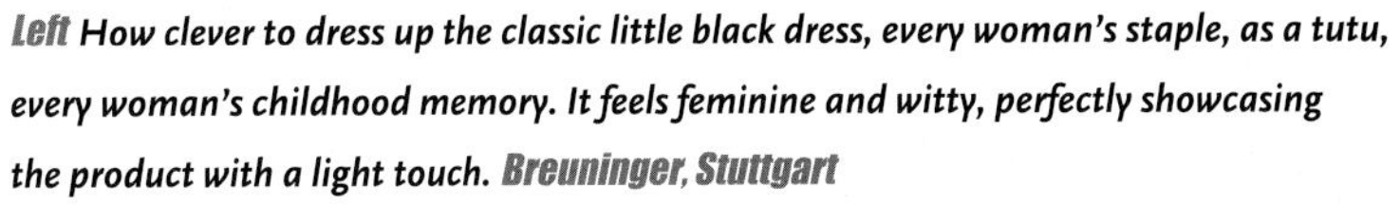

Left *How clever to dress up the classic little black dress, every woman's staple, as a tutu, every woman's childhood memory. It feels feminine and witty, perfectly showcasing the product with a light touch.* **Breuninger, Stuttgart**

Below *Neatly placed shoes face in opposing directions with the grids upon which they're placed providing graphic relief and making shapes and patterns with shadows.* **Sergio Rossi, Milan**

Opposite above *Drenching the set in light and setting it against a pale backdrop to emphasize shadow makes a very moody, dramatic tableau. The glasses of red wine subtly reinforce the mood of an after-dark affair.* **Bergdorf Goodman, New York**

Opposite below *This curvaceous shape echoes the plunge from shoulder to waist of the female mannequins clothed in backless dresses, a display successful for its minimal and sensual restraint.* **Yati, New York**

Opposite *These days, the anatomy of a mannequin comes in a multitude of different finishes. These space-age versions by Bonaveri show that shop window design has already entered the twenty-first century.* ***Bonaveri***

Mannequins

'When you see them naked, there's not much difference in the size – they all look the same. But the difference is in what their figures are saying to you – it's all about body language.'

Michael Southgate, Adel Rootstein

Each generation has touchstones – from cars to shoes, pop icons to puddings – that capture the essence of the moment. The Sixties had the Mini Cooper, Mary Quant and The Beatles. Platform shoes, discos and Black Forest gateau sum up the Seventies, and shoulder pads, logos and Porsches all recall the Eighties. Each marker is peculiar to its own generation and an anathema to the next, as the urge to forge ahead finds form in the vagaries of popular culture, from fashion to music to beauty. But unlike the infinity of numbers, fashions repeat themselves with almost seasonal regularity – the soundtracks of generations separated by thirty years are reunited as the melodic strains of The Beatles echo in those of Oasis. But although Kate Moss picks up where Twiggy left off as the face and shape of a waif generation, the two could never be mistaken for sisters, even when scrubbed of make-up, wearing plain black dresses and with their hair in a ponytail – their body language defines the eras of their catwalk reigns quite distinctly.

Flick through the pages of *Vogue* and the photography and the models' poses define each era as much as the clothes. In the Fifties, the Mayfair Slump was as much a phenomenon of the times as the New Look, when narrow skirts with tight nipped-in jackets saw models limp along with their stomachs held in and their shoulders rounded over. In the Sixties, everything was far freer. The doe-eyed dollybird dressed in a mini and pumps alternately sat languid and long, like a rag doll, or jumped in the air with childlike vigour, either way preaching that dewy youth was forging the revolution. In each instance, the spirit of the moment manifested itself physically through body language.

In corporate fields, too, body language is regarded as a vital tool that sells interviewees at interviews, with research showing that approximately 90% of an interviewer's analysis is based on non-verbal communication alone, so it follows that the body language of mannequins in a window can do the same. By investing the merchandise with the moment's attitude and verve, the mannequin mimics the customer's aspirations, whilst working within the images of the retailer and the designer label. The mannequin takes on the face of the moment and reflects it back through the glass of shop windows.

Michael Southgate, Creative Director of the mannequin manufacturers Adel Rootstein, explains: 'Very often expression is there in the hands. If the pose is very simple and relaxed, then the hand is; if there's life and vitality, then there's action in the hand, and if the product calls for sophistication, then it's shown through very spiky hands. Hands change as much as faces do, but even then it's more a matter of the tilt of the head than the face that keeps in the body language of the figure. The fundamental form of mannequins over the past decades has changed remarkably little. Yes, the hand may be tense, or the bust may be higher, but they're always a size 8–10. It's only the attitude, the atmosphere they create, that changes. Rootstein produce a line of figures called Partners. They're multi-racial and absolutely straight up and down because there aren't the clothes around now that can handle the dramatic poses. Fashion is no longer about that. According to how you are dressed you move and act differently, and no one's walking down the catwalk with great attitude; models today wander on looking about and pretending the audience isn't there, and it suits the clothes. When we did the sketches of the mannequins from the shows they all looked so boring and yet the shows hadn't been at all. We realized that it was because occasionally the models would hold hands, they were black, white, Asian, and that was what made it "today". It used to be about the brightness of the lipstick and the length of the false eyelashes – now it's a different kind of drama.'

Mannequins are far more than just a torso and limbs. To trace their chronology is to chart a course through the history of fashion and modern popular culture. In Paris in the 1950s, display artists perfected the art of laying the clothes flat in the window, a technique which became known as Paris Display. There were breathtaking displays at Hermès and particularly Christian Dior, where the merchandise – the scarf, the dress, the earrings, the shoes – would be grouped around a prop or a small fantasy figure in the centre. Everything was coordinated, in the spirit of the fashions at the time, and it was a look all its own. But then two things happened. The influence of the young teachers who went into the colleges after the Second World War and taught a lack of convention finally bore fruit, and a new scene started to rise up from the street. Southgate explains: 'There was such a programmed way of thinking about fashion up to the 1950s. Paris was the queen and what she said, you did, and what *Vogue* said, you did. It was so simple. People were aghast if you wore last season's clothes – there really was such a thing as that.' But the new names challenged that and by the early 1960s, the coordinated look was over. At the same time, with fashion running in tandem with the music scene, the New York press coined the concept of Swinging London. 'Londoners didn't know they were swinging until the New York press told them; they thought they were struggling – it's all about perspective.' The American department stores sent their buyers over to see what the press were writing about and found a run of little lock-up shops at the back of Regent Street. The designers – Sol Tuppin, Zandra Rhodes, Ossie Clark, Jean Varon, among others – were renting their own spaces to sell their designs because they couldn't get floor space in the department stores. The American department stores bought up all their designs, precipitating the fame of what was to become the world-renowned Carnaby Street.

At that time, most mannequins throughout the world were American – wonderful, elegant, horsey ladies, stylized to a degree that they were extra-angular and extra-haughty, showing to perfection the socialite's Chanel suit with handbag and matching earrings. But when the new young styles from the young British designers were put on these mannequins, the image jarred. Says Southgate, 'They looked ridiculous in a mini-skirt or hotpants or kaftan; that wasn't anything to do with what they were all about – the mannequins revolted! It was crystal clear to Adel that we should be making mannequins of the people who were making London swing, so we did Patti Boyd, who actually married one of The Beatles, Sandy Shaw, barefoot, and then this extraordinary young girl, knock-kneed with make-up like no-one had ever seen before, who became known to the world as Twiggy.' They were the spirits of the 1960s who led the breakaway from the stylized mannequin and introduced the concept of models with 'character'. It wasn't just about showing the clothes now – it was about showing how to wear them and be a part of the scene. This brought its own problems. 'Towards the end of that period, the rise of "burning your bra" feminism gave rise to the trend for sheer fashions, so we had to put nipples on the mannequins. It gave us a lot of trouble, in the States especially, and we received calls from display teams saying they'd received mannequins with nipples on and had been ordered by their MDs to saw them off!'

In the 1970s, new ideas for the placement of mannequins came to the fore. In New York, Colin Birch at Bloomingdale's moved away from the norm of supporting the mannequins by a rod or wire and instead started to place them against a window or wall where they would lounge and lean against the glass, looking out at passers-by and initiating an interaction. It made a change and evolved into 'Street Theatre'. Candy Pratts, also at Bloomingdale's, once did a tableau set in an English gentlemen's club – all oak and Old Master oils. There was a row of girls sitting on chairs in dresses with chiffon points on the hem and a row of men standing behind them in First World War uniforms. It was a period window and very effective, but what made it dynamic was that the mannequins were all black – that gave it the edge.

Within a decade everything had moved on again. The influence of films such as *American Gigolo* brought fashion to the masses and made designers like Giorgio Armani and Calvin Klein household names. The emerging androgyny of these fashions, typified by the Armani suit, saw mannequins modelled with a square shoulder, a flat bust and narrow hips. Hollywood turned fashion into a global industry. Just as designers started opening boutiques worldwide and launching diffusion lines, the cult of the supermodel was born, bringing a curvier silhouette more pin-up than clothes-horse.

But when the world was hit by recession at the end of the 1980s, retailing was the first casualty. The dynamic, go-getting mannequin was quickly replaced with bust forms which spelt out moderation and simplicity. Japan particularly excelled at this minimalism. 'They would spotlight a dress between cement walls and a cement floor, with no stock or props anywhere and the sheer drama of it would be breathtaking,' remembers Southgate. The product would be presented as a work of art, but quietly so; the flashy, brassy mannequin was a thing of the past.

That subtler approach is with us still. The mid-1990s resurgence of London, the capital of Cool Britannia, and the blossoming of designer boutiques the length of Madison Avenue are localized examples of the boom retailers have experienced in the past few seasons, but if consumption, particularly of luxury goods, has soared, it is with a low profile. Definitions of taste have changed along with fashions, and now cashmere is in and gilt'n'quilting is out. The New York department store Neiman Marcus is the master of the softly-softly approach. Mannequins are placed looking at the merchandise, perhaps standing at the edge of the rail or looking in a mirror with their backs to the customer, in a much softer sell. They're styled to fit in, to look at the same things as the customer, and not be stared at themselves.

These soft-sell mannequins are supported by props which create a domestic atmosphere that presents the shop as a home that just happens to sell things. Paul Smith's new store in London's Westbourne Grove is the epitome of this trend, placing products in a house and selling in the drawing room and the kitchen. The concept of the store is changing, and so is the role of the mannequin. As shopping malls continue to flourish, they propagate the 'open set' trend where the pedestrian can look through the windows into the store, something which places a new, stronger accent on interiors. Joseph has spearheaded this approach to startling effect, taking mannequins from the windows into the store, perhaps on the stairs or by the changing rooms. Bloomingdale's has also linked windows and in-store spaces by placing mannequins in the middle of gangways. They are set by foot spigots and have no visible means of support, so that once people start to mill around the store, the mannequins become part of the crowd, their poses as natural and relaxed as the customers'. Such a use of the mannequin as an interactive marketing tool runs in tandem with retailing's other intiatives to woo the customer who, saturated with the modern media's advertising, promotions and marketing exercises, expects more than a mannequin standing irrelevantly on a podium. The novelist Jay McInerney sums it up: 'I believe that the model represents the apex of millennial, postmodern society. We project onto them and ask them to represent for us. It's pure image, uncomplicated by content. Except for the simple message: "You want this."'

Opposite *A clever juxtaposition of chic clothes and rebellious, punk mannequins by Adel Rootstein with spectacular eyelashes and Mohican hairstyles makes the products doubly striking.*

Above left, centre and right *Mannequins come in all colours, shapes and sizes. The grey, sculpted look on the left is very striking, while the interaction of two mannequins, centre, can create visual stories. The relaxed, supermodel pose of the right-hand mannequin comes straight from the catwalk.*
Saks, San Francisco (left); I. Magnin, San Francisco (centre and right)

Above left *This mannequin's pose conveys attitude which helps to establish the brand's aspirations.* **Saks, Beverly Hills**

Above centre and right *Torso mannequins, having no personality of their own, will never replace their fully grown cousins, but they're well-suited to windows in which one garment or accessory is being promoted.*
Lagerfeld, Paris (centre); Saks, Houston (right)

Above left *Mannequins can be used to invite interaction with passers-by, but be careful that the effect isn't mannered.* **Dickins & Jones, London**

Above centre *Interaction between mannequins, unless very original and cleverly managed, can seem dated.* **Heinemann, Düsseldorf**

Above left *The bust is a useful device for display in the smaller window. Here, a richly coloured and patterned tie is set off by the luxurious, masculine sobriety of a leather sofa.* **Lagerfeld, Paris**

Above left and right *These beautiful and very expensive mannequins by Adel Rootstein have been given complete makeovers. Their hair has been styled, their faces made up, and their clothes coordinated to the limit for maximum effect.*

Above left *The natural energy of the pose invites a response, and shows off the cut of the clothes to active young customers who will identify with the look.* **Saks Fifth Avenue, New York**

Above right *Interaction between mother and child is completely absent in this example by Almax Mannequins: in my view baby mannequins are at their best when naively unrealistic.*

COSTUME
CROISÉ
980
CHEMISE
435
CRAVATE
100

bollé
bollé
bollé
WOMEN'S WEAR
THE
EXCLUSIVE
OILILY

INSPIRATIONAL WINDOWS

The following list of stores where innovative shop-window design can regularly be seen is a personal selection of favourites from the many wonderful designs in this book.

ABC Carpet
888 Broadway
New York, NY 10003

Bergdorf Goodman
754 Fifth Avenue
New York, NY 10019

Bloomingdale's
1000 Third Avenue
New York, NY 10022

Citarella
2135 Broadway
New York, NY 10023

Dickins & Jones
244 Regent Street
London W1A 1DB

French Connection
249 Regent Street
London W1R 7AD

Gucci
32–33 Old Bond Street
London W1X 4HH

Habitat
196 Tottenham Court Road
London W1P 9LD

Harvey Nichols and Co. Ltd
109–125 Knightsbridge
London SW1X 7RJ

Heal's
196 Tottenham Court Road
London W1P 9LD

Hermès
42 Avenue George V
75008 Paris

Jigsaw
126–127 New Bond Street
London W1Y 9AF

Liberty Plc
214 Regent Street
London W1R 6AH

Lord and Taylor
424 Fifth Avenue
New York, NY 10018

Marshall Field's
111 North State Street
Chicago, IL 60602

Neiman Marcus
1618 Main Street
Dallas, TX 75201

Paul Smith Ltd
40–44 Floral Street
London WC2E 9DG

Reiss
The Reiss Building
114–116 King's Road
London SW3 4TX

Selfridges and Co.
400 Oxford Street
London W1A 1AB

ZCMI
2200 South 900 West
Salt Lake City, UT 84137

pp.102 and 123. Marshall Field's. Design Team, Holiday Windows-Store for Men *(p.102),* Flowering Field's *(p.123): Jamie Becker, Director of Visual Marketing, Dayton Hudson. Amy Meadows, Visual Merchandising Manager, State Street. Steve Didier, Window Display Manager, State Street. p.102: Kevin Grace, Designer.*

DIRECTORY OF SUPPLIERS

Laminates

A&D Display
3 Cross Street
Suffern
New York, NY 10901

Abet Ltd
70 Roding Road
London E6 4LS

Perstorp Warerite Ltd
Aycliffe Industrial Park
Newton Aycliffe
County Durham DL5 6EF

Gooding Aluminium Ltd
1 British Wharf
Landmann Way
London SE14 5RS

Formica Ltd
Coast Road
North Shields
Tyne and Wear NE29 8RE

Lighting

Aktiva Ltd
(ambient and display lighting)
10B Spring Place
London NW5 3BH

Concord Lighting Ltd
174 High Holborn
London WC1V 7AA

Erco Lighting Ltd
38 Dover Street
London W1X 3RB

Iguzzini Lighting UK
Unit 3
Mitcham Industrial Estate
85 Streatham Road
Mitcham
Surrey CR4 2AP

Isometrix Lighting and Design
8 Glasshouse Road
London EC1A 4JN

Lumino Lighting
Lumino House
Lovet Road
Harlow
Essex CM19 5TB

SKK Lighting
34 Lexington Street
London W1R 3HR

SLD Lighting
318 West 47TH Street
New York, NY 10036

Mannequins

Almax International SpA
PO Box 97
Via Boaresco 44
22066 Mariano Comense
Italy

Bertenstein Display
138 West 25TH Street
5TH Floor
New York, NY 10001

Bodyline
Unit 16
The Aberdeen Centre
22 Highbury Grove
London N5 2DQ

Bonaveri Manichini srl
Via Ariosto 9
44042 Cento
Italy

Gemini Mannequins Ltd
51 Mortimer Street
London W1N 7DT

Heiwa Mannequin Co. Ltd
1-17-9 Kitaohsuka
Toshima-Ku
Tokyo 170
Japan

Hindsgaul Mannequins A/S
Maaloev Byvej 19–23
2760 Maaloev
Denmark

Hindsgaul
Unit 13
Liddall Way
Horton Road
West Drayton UB7 8PG

Kyoya Co. Ltd
1-8-12 Yakuin
Chuo-Ku
Fukuoka 810
Japan

Patina-V
15650 Salt Lake Avenue
City of Industry, CA 91745

Proportion London Ltd
9 Dallington Street
London EC1V OLN

Pucci Mannequins
44 West 18TH Street
12TH Floor
New York, NY 10011

Adel Rootstein Ltd
Shawfield House
Shawfield Street
London SW3 4BB

Sperling Models Ltd
36 Hollands Road
Haverhill
Suffolk CB9 8PR

Miscellaneous

Amari Plastics
2 Cumberland Avenue
London NW10 7RL

Bollom Paint Centre
71 Brushfield Street
London E1 6AA

Borovick Fabrics Ltd
(display fabrics)
16 Berwick Street
London W1V 4HP

B. Brown Displays
74–78 Wood Lane End
Hemel Hempstead
Hertfordshire HP2 4RF

Creative Arts Unlimited
(props)
3730 Seventieth Avenue North
Pinellas Park, FL 33781

George Dell
(Christmas decorations)
151 West 25th Street
New York, NY 10001

Ells & Farrier
(beads, sequins and thread)
20 Beak Street
London W1R 3HA

Inflate Ltd
(inflatable product design)
Third Floor
5 Old Street
London EC1V 9HL

Pilkington Glazing
Unit 26
Bermondsey Trading Estate
Rotherhithe New Road
London SE16 3LE

J. Preedy & Sons Ltd
(glass merchants)
Stanley Works
7B Coronation Road
London NW10 7PQ

Propaganda
(props and artwork)
138 West 25th Street
9th Floor
New York, NY 10001

Seven Continents
(forms, fixtures and furniture)
138 West 25th Street
2nd Floor
New York, NY 10001

RETAIL DESIGN

Umdasch Shop-Concept
(shop-fitting)
Reichsstrasse 23
3300 Amstetten
Austria

Vitrashop Ltd
(shop-fitting and fixture design)
Bedford Avenue
Slough
Berkshire SL1 4RY

Yellow Door
22–24 Torrington Place
London WC1E 7HJ

FURTHER READING

Simon Doonan
Confessions of a Window Dresser
New York, 1998

Peter Dormer
Design Since 1945
London and New York, 1993

Rodney Fitch
Fitch on Retail Design
London, 1990

Wally Olins
Corporate Identity
London, 1989

Martin M. Pegler
Store Windows
New York, 1998

Sylvio Sanpietro, ed.
Made in Italy: New Shops 5
New York, 1998

Mitzi Sims
Sign Design: Graphics, Materials, Techniques
London, 1991

Andrew Tucker
The London Fashion Book
London and New York, 1998

Winning Shopping Center Designs 5
The International Council of Shopping Centers
New York, 1999

JOURNALS

Inspiration

Red

Visual Merchandising and Store Design